THE CRITICAL LINK

COMMUNITY

COLLEGES

AND THE

WORKFORCE

Lisa Falcone, Editor

A project of the American Association of Community Colleges

with funding from the U.S. Department of Labor

WORKPLACE DEVELOPMENT PROJECT
Lynn Barnett, Project Director
Lisa Falcone, Project Manager

THE CRITICAL LINK:
Community Colleges and the Workforce
Lisa Falcone, Editor

This publication has been prepared under Grant No. F-4006-2-00-80-60 from the U.S. Department of Labor, Employment and Training Administration, awarded to the American Association of Community Colleges. The contents do not necessarily reflect the views of the U.S. Government, nor does mention of any products or organizations imply endorsement by the U.S. Government.

American Association of Community Colleges
National Center for Higher Education
One Dupont Circle, N.W., Suite 410
Washington, DC 20036

T A B L E   O F   C O N T E N T S

P R E F A C E

 merica's 1,200 community colleges are vital to the national effort to train and retrain this country's workforce for higher-skill, higher-wage jobs. Community colleges are accessible to virtually every American, both in terms of geographical location and of their mission to provide lifelong learning for any adult who desires additional training. Employers, regardless of type or size, frequently select community colleges as a regular source of technical training on workplace education. Workers can turn to community colleges to upgrade existing skills and/or learn new skill areas.

The critical link of any community college workforce training program is the professional staff who develop quality training in partnership with government, business, and labor. Often called business/industry liaisons, these community college professionals are integral to the nation's quest to keep America's people working. For this reason, in 1993, AACC targeted business/industry liaisons for a series of professional development initiatives. The information learned from these initiatives serves as the cornerstone of this publication.

AACC wishes to thank the U.S. Department of Labor, Employment and Training Administration, for providing the primary source of funds to support both the workplace development project and this publication. AACC also extends appreciation to the National Institute for Technology Training for assisting with planning and implementation of the Workplace Development Institute. Most importantly, AACC commends the many community college business/industry liaisons who through their work make it possible for numerous Americans to receive the necessary skills and consequently the self-confidence to lead more productive and higher quality lives.

David Pierce
President
American Association of Community Colleges
February 1994

I N T R O D U C T I O N

 n 1993, the American Association of Community Colleges actively supported and assisted community colleges nationwide in their efforts to provide workforce training services to employees of small and medium-sized businesses and industries. AACC sponsored five activities, all of which were designed to build the capacity of community colleges to respond effectively to workforce development needs of employers and employees through contract training services.

Three of these activities were professional development initiatives that targeted community college-based business/industry liaisons, individuals who are the critical link between community colleges and their local business communities. Business/industry liaisons coordinate the needs assessments of businesses and the necessary training to improve the skill level of workers.

The professional development initiatives were: (1) a national conference called the Workforce Development Institute; (2) a survey of Institute participants; and (3) five regional forums. Through these initiatives, AACC found that professional development is vital to business/industry liaisons because of the uniqueness of their jobs at community colleges. One Institute participant said, "The chance to meet and discuss workforce issues and training techniques with other professionals from across the country is invaluable to the services I provide back home."

Directly related to these initiatives were two other workforce activities: (1) a policy statement about the role of community colleges in providing workforce training; and (2) a project in which AACC identified "new work" occupations that require no more than two years of postsecondary training.

Developed jointly with the League for Innovation in the Community College and adopted by AACC's Board of Directors in August 1993, the policy paper, *The Workforce Training Imperative: Meeting the Training Needs of the Nation,* provides a plan of action for community colleges, businesses and industries, and local, state, and federal governments. It serves as a roadmap for implementation of workforce policies.

Through the "new work" project, AACC identified 35 occupations that are considered to be post-industrial, higher-skilled, and higher-wage. The jobs require two years or less of postsecondary education and serve as examples of occupational training that community colleges should be providing so that graduates will have a better than average opportunity for employment.

This publication was produced to share the input of community college business/ industry liaisons from across the country who participated in one or more of the workplace development initiatives. It also includes selected articles, an excerpt from AACC's policy paper, and new work occupation descriptions.

W O R K P L A C E
D E V E L O P M E N T
I N I T I A T I V E S

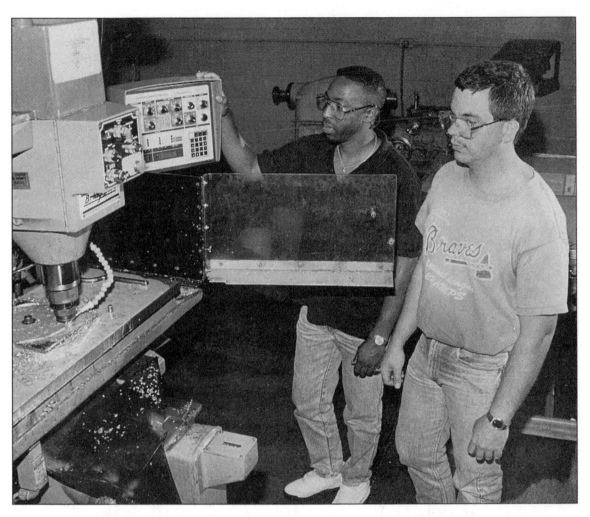

Students participate in the Machine Tool Technology Program at Calhoun Community College, Alabama. Photo credit: John Godbey

W O R K P L A C E

D E V E L O P M E N T

I N I T I A T I V E S

Workplace Development Institute

n February of 1993, AACC sponsored the Workplace Development Institute in Nashville, Tennessee. Designed as a national training conference for community college business/ industry liaisons, the Institute was planned in collaboration with the National Institute for Technology Training. The impetus for the Institute was the position of community colleges as logical providers of workforce training for the nation's businesses and industries. They are well-positioned in their communities to develop partnerships with local businesses and to assist small and medium-sized companies reinvest in themselves, their employees, and the economic vitality of their regions.

Presenters from business, education, and government provided participants with training and resources to help them do a better job delivering services to businesses, particularly small and medium-sized firms. The Institute curriculum focused on local outreach, workforce literacy, needs assessment, technical training, and work restructuring.

Nearly 150 community college professionals from 26 states and the District of Columbia attended the Institute. Although their titles varied from vice president and dean of workforce education to workplace specialist, most participants serve as the direct link between community college services and the local business community's employee training and assessment needs.

The Workplace Development Institute received highly positive evaluations, with participants reporting that it was one of the few meetings organized specifically to help community college professionals improve customer training and industry linkages. The opportunity to network with professionals from other regions of the country was valued, as was the information provided to help train workers of small and medium-sized companies.

Section II of this publication contains selected articles written by Institute presenters.

Post-Institute Assessment

Following the Institute, AACC ascertained that its workplace training programs and resources were appropriate and beneficial to community college business/industry liaisons through two assessments. The first was a follow-up survey of Institute participants; the second, a series of subsequent regional meetings, which included nearly 150 additional community college business/industry liaisons from selected areas of the country. The survey focused strictly on professional development needs of community college business/industry liaisons, whereas the regional meetings investigated the pressing issues affecting effective workforce training.

Although the number of people involved in the survey and regional meetings was relatively small, the responses were overwhelmingly consistent. The information generated from both the survey and regional forums serves as an indicator of the professional development needs and concerns of community college business/industry liaisons nationwide.

Workplace Development Institute Survey

The survey was sent to Workplace Development Institute participants five months after the conference. A cover letter explained that the survey was designed to generate information about their practical applications of workforce training and assessment. AACC wanted to know if the Institute made a difference in the operations of the participants' workforce training services. Specifically, they were asked to provide demographic information about their college workplace training programs; to comment about the Institute's training sessions that were most beneficial and applicable to their jobs; and to describe types of training not offered at the Institute that would be useful in future professional development programs.

A total of 120 surveys were mailed to participants and 60 surveys (50 percent) were returned. Although this was a respectable rate of return, it likely would have been higher if the surveys had not been sent during the summer when some community colleges operate on a limited schedule, and many staff and administrators are away from campus.

Of those completing the survey, 58 percent described their campuses as rural, 29 percent as urban, and 27 percent as suburban (some responded to more than one classification because they represent multi-campus colleges).

The majority reported operating their business/industry training programs out of continuing education departments or independent business/industry centers. While the level of resources provided by institutions vary, most programs appear to operate with minimal resources, including staff. Some reported they are completely self-sustaining programs.

When asked to categorize the skills training provided to business and industry, the respondents reported the following:

- 91 percent computer

- 90 percent technical

- 79 percent team building

- 75 percent workplace literacy

- 7 percent quality assurance

- 10 percent supervision.

The colleges surveyed also reported providing some training to workers in companies of all sizes: 85 percent reported training workers in small companies (under 50 employees); 100 percent, in medium-sized companies (50 to 500 employees); and 79 percent, in large companies (more than 500 employees).

Institute training sessions in workplace literacy, contracts, industry networks, total quality management (TQM), economic development, and marketing training programs were rated as the most useful by participants. Also highly rated were ISO 9000, just-in-time training, and technical presentations.

When asked for specific examples of how sessions benefited their training services, some Institute participants responded that they had:

- implemented a small business consortium with the local chamber of commerce to address the needs of the small business community;

- improved contract procedures;

- made an informed decision about whether to join the state consortium and deliver ISO 9000 training;

- added a workplace literacy component to their services.

There were many different responses to a question regarding the areas in which additional training would be desirable. The most commonly cited answers were: assessment of business and industry needs, resource collaborations, writing and applying for grants, and pricing structures. Some others said the sessions offered at the Institute were right on target, but they need more in-depth training in areas such as contracts, developing networks, marketing training programs, workplace literacy programs, and total quality management.

Overall the survey responses demonstrated an ongoing demand for professional development opportunities including, but not limited to, conferences and regional meetings. Most said developing networks with colleagues both regionally and nationally would be useful to them, particularly since many are the only persons on their campuses who work directly with the local business community. Professional training for faculty was deemed essential for community colleges to successfully move from traditional vocational education to workforce training.

Lack of funds was cited as the primary reason that more respondents have not attended other professional development programs. As community colleges tightened their overall budgets, professional development monies have become scarce. More than half of the participants of the Workplace Development Institute received scholarships, making it accessible to many who otherwise would not have attended.

Workplace Development Regional Forums

During the fall of 1993, representatives from AACC and the U.S. Department of Labor travelled to five areas of the country to conduct regional meetings with community college business/industry liaisons and presidents. Face-to-face discussions with professionals in the field produced information about local concerns and ideas for delivering effective training services, particularly to workers in small and medium-sized companies. The meeting format allowed participants to delve more deeply into pertinent issues than a written survey would permit.

The selected sites for the regional meetings were Bunker Hill Community College, Massachusetts; Fullerton College, California; Shoreline Community College, Washington; Parkland College, Illinois; and Brookhaven College, Texas. The sites were chosen based on geographical location, economic condition of the region, perceived level of training provided by the area community colleges, and types of business and industry based in the region.

Invitations were extended to community college presidents and business/industry liaisons located within an approximate three-hour driving radius of the selected sites. About 25 community college representatives attended each meeting. Eighty community colleges from 10 states were represented, with a relatively equal distribution of participants overall from rural, urban, and suburban areas.

At each meeting, AACC and DOL staff presented information about national programs, policies, and legislation that directly affect the linkage between community colleges and local companies. Each participant had an opportunity to share the strengths and limitations of his or her own program. In addition, the groups discussed the kind and level of assistance, training, and information they needed to be more effective in their jobs.

Overall, participants reported that they provide training for a wide variety of skill areas, including computer, technical, workplace literacy, team building, supervisory, communications, total quality management, and ISO 9000. Almost all reported the training they offer business and industry is customized for workers in individual companies.

Probably the most striking observation from the regional meetings was the similarity of concerns and needs of the participating colleges. This is not to say that there were no differences; there were, particularly the age and experience level of programs. Some community colleges have been offering contract training services to local business and industry for more than 20 years. Others are just beginning to establish contact with their local business communities. Some regions have established regional networks that appear to have a direct impact on the quality of training services they provide; others have limited or no existing network opportunities.

At all five regional forums, four issues were raised repeatedly by participants as their most pressing concerns about the effective delivery of workforce services. They were:

- funding resources, particularly for training in small and medium-sized companies;

- workplace literacy skills;

- community college image;

- training for existing jobs.

Funding

Most participants said that they provide some training to workers in small and medium-sized companies. The most notable exceptions were participants from southern California, who were more accustomed to working with large companies. However, because of the major economic shift in the number, size, and types of industry in their region, they are beginning to provide limited training to workers of small and medium-sized firms. They cited the cost of training and the inability of smaller firms to pay for training services as the primary reasons for not providing more contract training to workers of smaller companies.

Participants from other regions agreed. They said customized training is expensive. However, in Illinois, Washington, and Massachusetts, many colleges have already developed or are in the process of developing consortium approaches to training, which are an effective way to provide training to workers in smaller companies without bankrupting either the participating businesses or community colleges.

Knowing how to apply for local, state, and federal workforce training funds was another issue for some participants. Many were often unaware of grants and other government assistance for which they might be eligible to apply. Still others expressed concern that the monies they do receive from government are typically restricted for training programs only and cannot be used for equipment. Such restrictions make it difficult to provide effective training where it is most needed. One participant said, "We can't train for state-of-the-market technologies with old equipment."

Because many community college workforce training programs are totally self-sustained, and some may even support other community college programs, many participants referred to the "cash cow dilemma." The challenge is deciding whether to provide programs needed by the community or to offer programs that generate money for the college.

Several participants asked for help identifying where resources can be accessed. Grant-writing training, regular information about grant applications and deadlines, and consortia-building models would be helpful in improving the resource and funding predicament. They asked that a national database for community college workforce service providers include accurate information about funding sources.

Workforce Literacy Skills

In some regions, participants were greatly concerned about the skill level of the workers being trained. As one participant put it, "The basic skill level of many of the workers is woefully inadequate and must be addressed before attempting to train for high-skill technology positions."

Washington state community colleges, in particular, reported a high demand for literacy training. Assessment of skill levels of workers needs to be done before they can be effectively placed for more advanced training. Interest was expressed in development of a curriculum prototype for community colleges nationwide to use in basic skills training as a cost-effective approach. Information on curriculum models for workplace readiness skills in reading, writing, communication, and math could be made available through a national community college workforce database.

Community College Image

Although community colleges as a whole are ready and able to provide training services to business and industry, some members of the business community simply are not aware that these programs exist in their own backyards. Many participants said marketing their programs was a difficult task, as businesses often look to traditional service providers such as private consultants before turning to community colleges for training. Even though community colleges are evolving into major providers of high-skill training and are playing a significant role in the vitality of local economies, some businesses as well as the general public do not know about these changes. Some participants said, "Community colleges are the best kept secret in their regions."

In addition, some businesses have not bought into the concept that training will improve their overall productivity and success. They do not see training as an investment, but rather as an unnecessary expense. College participants at all five regional meetings asked for a national public relations campaign that highlights the changing role of community colleges, particularly regarding economic development and training.

Training for Existing Jobs

The most critical issue raised by participants of the regional forums was the increase in laid-off workers and the lack of jobs. The comment, "You can't train people for jobs that do not exist anymore," was echoed throughout the forums.

The need is critical for community colleges to provide training for jobs that exist in today's economy and will still be viable in the future. Many states have seen the collapse of businesses and industries. In some areas, thousands of jobs have been lost. Finding new jobs to replace the old ones is a crucial issue, and identifying new industries is essential.

Community colleges must be able to link effectively their training with real jobs. Accurate national and regional projections for occupational trends and worker skills are needed. Community colleges must be at the table with business and regional and state officials when trying to attract new industries to their regions. In addition, community colleges must conduct assessments of their own service areas so that they know the changing needs of local businesses and can provide appropriate skill training to meet those needs.

Participants asked for help determining skills that are needed now and will be needed in the future by workers. Community colleges must take a futuristic approach in their assessments if the training they provide is to make a positive difference in the lives of their students.

The National Role

The regional forums provided AACC and DOL representatives an opportunity to hear directly the most pressing issues affecting community colleges in their role as provider of workforce training. These discussions confirmed that the workforce training provided by community colleges is critical to the nation's pursuit to ensure that every American who wants to work can. In addition, it was clear that community college workforce training service providers cannot do their very important work alone.

Community colleges, businesses and industries, and local, state, and federal governments must work together to ensure that the obstacles affecting effective workforce training
can be minimized or eliminated. In addition, they must look to collaboration on the development of curricula and workforce training services provided to America's workers to guar-
antee that the skills training offered is applicable and beneficial to both workers and employers. Joint efforts through consortia and networks are essential.

AACC can assist community colleges across the country by continuing to serve as a
national voice for community colleges in Congress and the White House. AACC can also
serve as a convener of training opportunities and help to keep the national network going
through improved information sharing.

Section III of this publication contains AACC's suggested plan of action for implementing a national workforce training system.

W O R K P L A C E
D E V E L O P M E N T
I N S T I T U T E :

Selected Articles

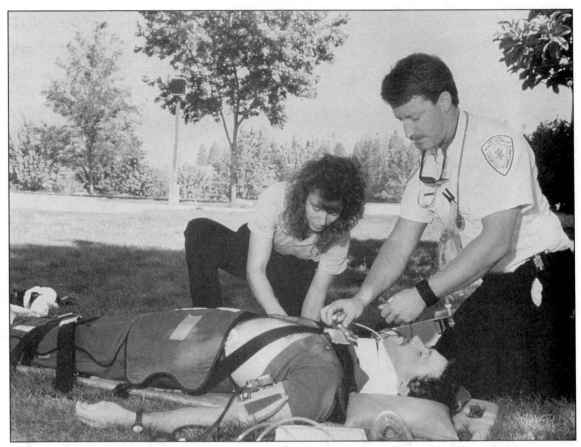

Crafton Hills College in California provides a regional training center for paramedics.
Photo credit: Paul Hayashi

INTRODUCTION TO ISO 9000

Harrison Wadsworth, Dennis Kelly and Larry Alford

ost small and mid-sized companies do not have a documented, demonstrable quality management system. Many managers erroneously believe that quality is achieved through strong admonitions to "do it right the first time." Excellent product and service quality, however, don't just happen. They are the result of a defined and implemented plan to manage all aspects of the business. The ISO 9000 series of international quality standards provides a structure on which to build an effective quality management system.

What Is ISO 9000?

The ISO 9000 series of standards is a family of documents developed by technical committees of the Geneva-based International Organization for Standardization. The objective of the ISO series is to establish internationally-acceptable quality system standards which (1) provide a management guideline to maintain the desired quality at an optimum cost, and (2) through compliance, create customer confidence in the company's ability to consistently deliver the desired quality performance.

More than 90 countries are active on these committees. At present, 60 nations have adopted the ISO standard as their national quality standard, including Japan and the United States. Two of the documents, ISO 9000 and 9004, are for internal use. ISO 9001, 9002 and 9003 are contractual documents to be used in meeting the quality assurance requirements of customers. In this country, the basic standards are referred to as ANSI/ASQC Q90, Q91, Q92, Q93 and Q94.

ISO 9000 provides guidelines for the selection and use of the most relevant contractual standard. ISO 9001 is the model for firms engaging in design, development, production, installation, and servicing activities. ISO 9002 is identical to 9001 but excludes the design function. ISO 9003 covers only final inspection and test activities. ISO 9004 is a guide for management in the development of an appropriate quality system.

Supplementary documents, including a terminology standard ISO 8402 (ANSI/ASQC A3), are in various stages of development. Others are ISO 9000-3 for software systems, ISO 9004-2 for service industries, ISO 9004-3 for processed materials, and ISO 9004-4 on quality improvement.

ISO standards are generic in that they apply to a wide variety of enterprises. They are not process, product or industry specific. Great latitude is given to management to design the most cost-effective system that meets the standard's requirements.

Audits Document Compliance, Registration Publicizes Compliance

The ISO standards were originally planned to involve only the firm that supplies goods or services and the purchaser of those goods and services. The manufacturer would perform internal audits to verify that its quality systems were working properly. The purchasing firm might elect to visit and perform an audit periodically.

This practice of second-party audits, where the buyer audits the provider's quality system, has been quite popular in the United States. The U.S. Department of Defense, automotive companies, and others have aggressive programs of auditing their suppliers. Companies with multiple customers might face several second-party audits each year. Each customer will likely compare the company's quality system to different quality standards.

The European Community (EC) suggested a different approach. The EC recognized that in an international market, continuing the practice of second-party audits would be expensive. It suggested the use of independent, third-party auditors to verify suppliers' compliance to ISO standards. As an independent auditor judged a firm to be in compliance, the auditor's organization (referred to as the Registrar) could certify or "register" the supplying firm's quality system. Therefore, the responsibility and cost of demonstrating quality system effectiveness was placed squarely on each supplying firm. Second-party audits, if still justified, could be performed on a reduced scale and frequency.

The "registered" firm is able to use the Registrar's logo on documents, advertisements, and correspondence to communicate its adherence to ISO standards. No mark is to be placed on any product. The registration applies to the *quality system* only. Once registered, the registrar will periodically revisit its client to audit for continued compliance.

Increasing Interest in ISO 9000

Interest in ISO standards is increasing rapidly. The 1990 EC decision to adopt ISO standards as a part of its product certification process fueled concerns that a company's failure to comply with ISO would eliminate access to European markets. Although it is true that a few regulated product areas will require compliance, most will not. However, regardless of regulation, any customer may demand compliance as part of the terms of a contract.

More than 12,000 firms in the United Kingdom are registered. As of January 1993, 715 American sites were registered. The United States is far behind at present, but the number of registered sites here is growing exponentially. A recent survey of Georgia exporters showed that 50 percent are interested in determining their companies' needs for ISO registration.

Experts believe that market forces will have the greatest impact on decisions to comply with the standards. These forces include (1) significant customer(s) who demand it, (2) competitive disadvantages from competitors who comply with ISO, and (3) a targeting of markets in which compliance will be important. Firms may pursue ISO compliance simply because an effective quality system will reduce waste, scrap and rework.

Implementing ISO 9000

How to begin

Begin by obtaining management commitment. Establish a steering committee with a qualified coordinator to identify what needs to be done. Provide the appropriate training. Evaluate your current quality system against the appropriate ISO standard's requirements. Identify shortfalls and define action plans to implement improvements.

Select a registrar

As a target date for the registration audit is set, select and contact a registrar. Some firms report waiting lists as long as six to twelve months. Choose a registrar based on its experience with your industry, on its ability to meet the defined schedule, and on recommendations from customers and industry contacts.

Prepare for registration

Preparing for registration requires documentation of the quality system in the form of (1) a quality manual, (2) work procedures and (3) work instructions. Train the organization on the new procedures. Begin performing internal audits and applying corrective action for improvement. Companies may perform a pre-assessment audit to identify weaknesses prior to the registration audit.

At the time of the registration audit, the auditors will first examine the quality system documentation to determine its compliance with the chosen ISO standard. If it complies, the auditors then simply verify that the company "does what it says it does." The registrars are not trying to fail companies. They are expected to maintain ethical and professional conduct and to faithfully uphold the integrity of the ISO standards. In fact, the registrars must be audited and accredited themselves by independent national accreditation bodies.

The Role of Higher Education

An American standard is being developed by the American Society for Quality Control for education and training institutions (ANSI/ASQC Z1.11). When completed, this document will put the ISO contractual standards in language that is commonly used in the education arena. This may provide a basis for registering educational institutions to the ISO 9000 standards.

In addition to implementing ISO as a means to improve the quality of education, many colleges, universities and technical centers could assist local companies in being aware of what ISO can do for them. The unique relationships between education and industry provide many opportunities to convey this knowledge.

For example, the Georgia Institute of Technology in Atlanta has established the Georgia Tech Center for International Standards & Quality (CISQ). Using linkages established between local firms and regional industrial assistance service providers, CISQ provides a broad array of services for companies in Georgia and throughout the Southeast. A complete series of training courses, both open-enrollment and in-plant, are available. Experienced CISQ engineers also provide baseline quality system audits and assist in evaluating a firm's approach to ISO 9000 compliance. A subscription referral service called SQUIRE provides access to the latest information available on EC standards, regulations, and product directives. CISQ has also played a key role, with a major utility, Georgia Power Company, in establishing an ISO 9000 user network where firms meet regularly to exchange information about ISO implementation.

ISO 9000 provides a good framework for companies to manage quality. This can have a strong positive impact on company profits, even if formal registration to ISO 9000 isn't a company goal. Education providers with credible outreach programs and expertise in ISO 9000 can improve the economic future of companies in their service region.

The authors are affiliated with Georgia Institute of Technology's Center for International Standards and Quality.

C O L L A B O R A T I V E
I N D U S T R Y
N E T W O R K S

David Goetsch

collaborative industry network is a group of mutually sup-portive companies, usually small or medium-sized compa-nies, the members of which work together to solve common problems and enhance competitiveness. Industrial network-ing is a European concept that was originally developed in Italy after World War II. It is now widely used throughout Europe. Denmark and Italy are countries most actively engaged in industrial networking.

The goal of a collaborative industrial network is to enhance the competitiveness of its individual members by working together in ways that make them all stronger. Examples of collaborative activities include: joint education and training, joint contracts, shared work, joint purchasing, joint marketing, shared personnel, and shared technology.

Community colleges can play a critical facilitating role in the formation of collaborative industry networks by doing any or all of the following: (1) bringing chief executive officers of companies in their districts together on neutral territory to discuss collaboration; (2) staffing the network and providing office space; (3) surveying individual companies to identify common problems and needs; (4) providing directly and/or brokering education, training, and technical assistance for network companies; and (5) creating a capabilities database that can serve as the basis for teaming arrangements and marketing programs for network companies.

One of the first collaborative industry networks in the United States was the Technology Coast Manufacturing and Engineering Network (TeCMEN) in Fort Walton Beach, Florida. Founded in 1989, TeCMEN consists of 30 small and medium-sized com-panies that pool their resources and work together to solve common problems and to

WHAT IS A COLLABORATIVE INDUSTRY NETWORK?

A collaborative industry network is a group of mutually supportive companies, the members of which work together to solve common problems and enhance competiveness. Examples of collaborative activities are:

• Joint education and training

• Joint contracts

• Shared work

• Joint purchasing

• Joint marketing

• Shared personnel (fee basis)

• Shared technology (fee basis)

enhance competitiveness. Joint activities include joint marketing, joint education and training, joint purchasing, and shared expertise. TeCMEN was founded by Okaloosa-Walton Community College and is operated as a joint project of the college and Okaloosa Economic Development Council.

TeCMEN's mission statement reads as follows: "The Technology Coast Manufacturing and Engineering Network is a promotional group organized for the purpose of enhancing the business climate of Okaloosa County through the association and marketing of its technology-based companies."

Inherent in the mission of TeCMEN are such activities as the following:

• Marketing the joint capabilities of member companies to government and commercial markets.

• Facilitating the teaming of member companies to undertake projects larger than any single member company could do alone.

COMMUNITY COLLEGE'S ROLE

Community colleges can play a critical facilitating role in the formation of collaborative industry networks by doing all or any part of the following:

- Bringing CEOs together on neutral territory to discuss collaboration.

- Staffing the network and providing office space.

- Surveying the individual companies to identify needs in such areas as technical assistance, education, and training.

- Providing and/or brokering education, training, and technical assistance.

- Creating a capabilities database that can serve as the basis for teaming arrangements and marketing programs.

- Enhancing the competitiveness of member companies through the sharing of expertise, resources, and risk and through joint education and training.

Working together, TeCMEN companies are able to offer capabilities in three broad areas: metal fabrication, electronics fabrication, and manufacturing services.

Metal fabrication capabilities resident in the network include the following: material forming, heat treatment, broaching, sawing, turning, boring, drilling, reaming, milling, grinding, electrical discharge machining, non-traditional machining, welding, cutting, mechanical fastening, brazing, soldering, adhesive joining, statistical process control, just-in-time manufacturing, robotics, and computer-aided design, engineering and manufacturing.

Electronic fabrication capabilities include the following: electronic assembly, wire harness and cable assembly, printed circuit board assembly, and electronic chassis assembly.

Manufacturing services include: system integration and refurbishment, nondestructive testing, mechanical testing, computer-aided process planning, manufacturing resource planning, stereolithography, three-dimensional computer modeling, factory and process simulations, reliability modeling, and cost/benefit modeling.

Because the companies that can benefit from forming collaborative industry networks are likely to see each other as competitors, bringing them together usually requires an organization that has credibility with the individual companies and is seen as a disinterested third party. A community college can be such an organization. As such it can play a critical role in facilitating the formation and operation of collaborative industry networks.

David Goetsch is provost of Okaloosa-Walton Community College in Florida and founder of the Technology Coast Manufacturing Network.

EDUCATION AND INDUSTRY:

KEY ELEMENTS OF THE

WORKPLACE TRAINING

CONNECTION

Kenneth Mussnug and Jerry Lyons

 ver the past few years, the nature of training in America has changed. In the past, training programs were designed for management only, but today training and retraining is for all employees. Forty-one million Americans were trained in 1992 at a cost of $45 billion.

In an effort to have a positive impact on the economic development of the region, Western Kentucky University (WKU) established its Center for Training and Development with a basic mission: *to support and promote regional economic development by training the workforce.*

About the Center's Training Programs

The center, which consists of a three-person staff and student workers, provides on-site contract training programs to a service area with nearly a 100-mile radius. Currently the center offers 147 training topics in six areas:

- Quality Assurance Training — 30 percent

- Supervision and Management Training — 18 percent

- Team Development — 36 percent

- Technical and Maintenance Training — 3 percent

- Health and Safety Training — 6 percent

- Computer Training — 7 percent

Center personnel meet with company representatives and design programs to accommodate their training needs. The programs are drawn from topics that are already taught on campus and are customized for the company. All training is designed to meet a specific company goal.

The majority of the training requested during the center's five years of operation has been for "people skills." Nearly all the training provided has been designed to change behaviors and attitudes. Only three percent of training requested has been for technical training. Center personnel have found training aimed at changing attitudes and behaviors produces the best productivity gains.

To increase productivity, the companies need to train large numbers of people in a short period of time. The center is designed to assist companies with this need. First the center's personnel conducts a no cost needs analysis. The center has 92 trainers currently available, all of whom are carefully selected for their expertise and their ability to work with adult learners. Of the 92 trainers, 90 are full-time WKU faculty and two are adjunct faculty. The trainers are critical to the success of the center and its ability to respond to local business/industry needs.

WKU Center trainers must:

Know their subject matter...
    not necessarily an expert but very knowledgeable;
    understands current trends of subject matter

Understand the audience...
    age, experience, work departments, work history, level of education, previous training
    experiences

Be well prepared...
    follows goals and objectives;
    remains focused on subject matter;
    understands where session fits in program

Have training experience in industry...
    uses on-the-job techniques;
    attends train-the-trainer programs

Be comfortable working with adults...
> uses high participatory techniques such as questions/answers, discussion, and activities

Display enthusiasm and excitement...
> is very active;
> uses humor tactfully;
> is genuine and interested in helping;
> shows concern and cares about people

Prepare training facilities for delivery...
> sets up in advance of participants

Use proper presentation skills...
> speaks clearly;
> uses acceptable verbal pace

Present concepts, ideas and facts...
> as supported by research and experience;
> keeps personal opinions to a minimum;
> does not discuss unions, management, delicate policies and salaries;
> does not "talk down" to participants;
> stimulates creative thinking

React to logistics of industrial training...
> adjusts to last-minute schedule changes;
> remains flexible and patient;
> works in make-shift classrooms;
> customizes session content;
> is willing to receive constructive criticism

Use a variety of instructional aids...
> is comfortable using video equipment and flip charts;
> explains diagrams, blueprints, chart tables and models

Have abilities to handle delicate situations...
> employee "gripe" sessions;
> boisterous and loud participants

To date, more than 43,000 employees have been trained through the center's 2,900 training sessions. All the training was evaluated and both the company and trainer received a summary evaluation for each session conducted.

Employees receive a certificate upon successful completion of a training program. None of the training is for university credit; it is all designed to meet a specific company training need.

Western Kentucky University offers its center for public service reasons only. Centers should keep costs to a break even level, because lower costs allow companies to provide more training for their employees. Centers should also maintain administrative support and avoid perception of competition.

K E E P   I T   P U B L I C   S E R V I C E

1. Keep costs to a break even level.
2. Maintain administrative support.
3. Avoid perception of competition.

Who Wins?

The benefits for this kind of training are shared by the company, college, trainer, and state. Companies that participate will see an increased skill level of their employees, an increased production, and better quality. The college will receive improved community and public relations and may find an increase in donations. The trainer will gain real world experience and applications, use life examples for student activities, and increase business contacts for research and publications. The state and region will gain a stable tax base from companies that locate or remain in the area because of the training opportunities for employees. Overall college business/industry training centers, if operated professionally and efficiently, are a win-win situation for all involved.

Kenneth Mussnug and Jerry Lyons are on the professional staff of the Center for Industry and Technology at Western Kentucky University.

THE SKILLS ENHANCEMENT

PROGRAM

Andrea Hughes

tawamba Community College (ICC), in cooperation with the State Board of Community and Junior Colleges, the Department of Economic and Community Development, and the Mississippi Governor's Office, offers a Skills Enhancement Program to assist business and industry with workforce improvement initiatives focused on basic reading, writing, mathematics, communications and critical thinking skills. A workforce specialist serves as the college liaison in designing and customizing a Skills Enhancement Program to meet the unique needs of a company.

The Skills Enhancement Program focuses on the development of basic academic skills needed to perform a task in a critical area of a firm. Relying on the company goals for the critical area, a workplace audit is conducted to determine the basic skills needed to perform a given task. From this task analysis, basic skills are identified and translated into a curriculum. The training program is organized, partnership agreements signed, faculty oriented, training delivered, and an evaluation conducted. Cost-benefit analysis can be provided if the company will furnish the appropriate data.

Firms interested in this type of training program contact the workforce specialist in the Industry Service Division of Itawamba Community College. A meeting can be scheduled between the workforce specialist and company representatives to explain the program in more detail or to discuss training needs. The meeting can take place at any site that is mutually agreeable.

Determination of Critical Area/Program Goals

Once a decision to participate in the program has been reached, company officials should be prepared to discuss areas within their company that could benefit from the program. Goals and objectives for the different areas should be highlighted in order that training can be tailored to the needs of each area. This information is then used by the workforce specialist to guide information collection, curriculum development, and implementation activities.

The Workplace Audit/Basic Skills Identification

Once the parameters for a skills enhancement program are defined, ICC's workforce specialist goes on-site and conducts a workplace audit in the areas to be included in the program. Company employees are asked to train the workforce specialist for the various jobs as if he/she were a new employee. During this process, complete and detailed notes are taken to establish the standard operating procedure for each job. Various documents used by the employee in performing the job are collected for use in the training program. The process is typed and returned to the employee for review and editing. Revisions are then made to the standard operating procedure as requested by the employee and/or company.

With standard operating procedures for various jobs, the basic skills and thinking skills contained in each step of performing the tasks are identified. For example, if an employee must calculate upper and lower tolerances from a blueprint, obviously the ability to add and subtract fractions or decimals is necessary in order to be able to perform that function, and is therefore a basic skill to that step of the task. This type of analysis is performed on the entire process and a list of basic skills developed for the various jobs included in the program.

Curriculum Design and Program Organization

The curriculum for the Skills Enhancement Program is developed around lists of basic skills identified from the workplace audits. If job classifications are similar and a master skills list can be developed, then the program may be designed around the master skills list. A "functional context" approach is used in designing the skills enhancement program curriculum. This simply means that if a job requires calculating upper and lower tolerances from a blueprint, then that is the context in which the skill will be taught in the curriculum. In many instances, actual work sheets from the company are integrated into the curriculum for maximum effectiveness. Pre-tests and post-tests for the program are developed at this time.

During the curriculum design stage of the program, company officials will be expected to complete internal program planning and organization. Issues like participant recruiting, screening, and selection should be dealt with and finalized. Tentative training schedules should be developed. Other company incentive programs or considerations should be addressed and resolved so training can begin upon completion of the curriculum.

Partnership Agreement

The partnership agreement is a document that simply states the responsibility of the company and the community college in delivering the training. ICC's workforce specialist drafts this agreement after the company and the college have generally agreed to the organization of training, a curriculum has been developed, and instruction is ready to begin.

Instruction

Instructor selection and orientation is the responsibility of the college. In many instances the workforce specialist collaborates with the company to identify the best possible instructor(s) for the program. Instructor orientation emphasizes the importance of associating classroom skills with actual job/task activities. Often instructors visit the job site to verify that the basic skills taught in the classes are being used properly in the workplace.

Basic skills instruction is delivered using a "functional context" approach to subject matter. Using a curriculum developed from the task analysis and agreed to by the company, appropriate materials and supplies are provided to a properly oriented instructor for the delivery of instruction. Instruction is offered on a schedule agreed to by the company, at a site agreed to by the company, and at a time convenient to the company and its employees. Upon completion of the training, participants are given certificates of completion to document their accomplishments in the program.

Evaluation

In order to verify its effectiveness, a program evaluation is conducted upon completion of training. A variety of methodologies are used in the evaluation process, and they include but are not limited to pre/post tests, entrance/exit forms, and participant/supervisor interviews. If the company is willing to provide other tangible data, a cost-benefit analysis can be performed on the training program.

Andrea Hughes is a workforce specialist for Itawamba Community College in Fulton, Mississippi.

MARKETING TRAINING

TO THE BUSINESS

COMMUNITY

Rand Johnson

Salt Lake Community College's Experience

Between 1988 and 1989, Salt Lake Community College (SLCC) provided just over $100,000 in contract training to area businesses. Two years later, it provided more than $2 million in contract training to business customers. Why did the amount of business change so dramatically?

The increase is directly attributed to improved marketing techniques employed by the college. Specifically, the college developed a new marketing strategy and video, implemented business forums, and improved the database for mailings to business customers and potential customers.

Marketing Strategy

Have our customers tell our story became the general marketing strategy of the college's Advanced Technology Center (ATC). The college staff used this approach when developing marketing tools and events to spread the word about ATC's services and to attract more area businesses as customers.

This marketing strategy was first tested when the college created a brief trigger film to promote ATC training services to local businesses. Titled *The Bottom Line*, the video features satisfied business customers telling their stories about working with the center. The message is serious, but presented in an upbeat and persuasive style. Featured in the film are chief executive officers and managers from McDonnell Douglas, Ford, Natter Manufacturing, and other companies. On tape, they provide articulate and enthusiastic endorsements for the center. The spontaneous comments were so good that the script was thrown away during the video production.

Using customers to tell the center's story was also the strategy behind the ATC Breakfast Forums. Designed as a series, the breakfast forums are scheduled six times per year. At each breakfast, a spokesperson from a partner company is invited to speak about an issue or practice at his or her company that may be of interest to other businesses in the community. Some topics presented to date include: Building a Dynamic Corporate Culture; Meeting Business Objectives through Employee Empowerment; High Productivity Work Organizations: How We Got Lean and Mean; and Quality Is More Than a Manual.

The breakfast forums typically run an hour and a half. The college president serves as official host and welcomes the group, and the vice president introduces the guest speaker. Members of the ATC team spread themselves among the participants and utilize the time to get to know the business people in attendance. Intentionally, the college's portion of the program is minimal.

When the speakers give their presentations at the breakfast forums, without exception, they address the value and quality of SLCC's customized training programs. These live colleague-to-colleague endorsements have had a positive impact. New contract training opportunities have emerged directly from all of the breakfast forums held to date.

In addition to the breakfast forums, the college instituted the CEO Breakfast Roundtable Series, which provide SLCC staff an opportunity to network with top level decision-makers and to obtain authoritative input on immediate business training requirements. The roundtables are organized by industry and are typically co-hosted by a partner company with credibility within the target industry. For example, the general manager of the local McDonnell Douglas plant co-hosted a recent aerospace executive roundtable.

During each roundtable, the college president and key college staff speak briefly about the range of college services available to business and industry. During the balance of the meeting, the group openly discusses concrete ways the college can provide better services to targeted businesses. At a biomedical roundtable, the group identified a need to conduct a training-related needs assessment of Utah's biomedical industry. As a result, a survey was developed by the center's staff with help from several executives who attended the roundtable. SLCC is using the results of the survey to guide course development in the biomedical field.

Direct Mail Advertising

Another important component to the center's marketing strategy is a topnotch database system. On the college staff is a full-time graphic design and commercial art professional who develops promotional brochures, press releases, and other marketing materials aimed at the business community. The marketing materials are highly professional and look beautiful. However, without a quality, up-to-date database, the marketing materials use to have limited impact on generating business for the college.

Recognizing this problem, the Advanced Technology Center systematically developed a database designed to support direct mail advertising. The database is connected to the administrative mainframe and is accessible to those with appropriate clearance. It contains information on both customers and potential customers. The information is derived from a number of sources including: Utah's Department of Community and Economic Development, Economic Development Corporation of Utah, local trade associations, and customers who utilize the college training services. The information is updated on an ongoing basis, a process that requires commitment, time, and resources. For SLCC, the returns on this investment have been significant. There has been an increase awareness of programs and courses, particularly first-time programs that previously required more than one introduction to the market before they were successful.

Know Your Market

One other key to a successful marketing strategy is to know your market. Marketplace assessments conducted in a variety of ways, including telephone surveys, direct mail surveys, and personal interviews have become an integral part of the center's marketing system.

Surveys are developed with help and input from the college's industry partners. When administering a survey, the center staff emphasizes the college's desire to be flexible and to respond to the needs of the business community. The results are frequently used to identify the need for new course offerings. Information generated from surveys is often used by college staff when making follow-up calls on businesses.

Utah's Best Kept Secret

SLCC's former college president summed it up best when he said, "Salt Lake Community College is Utah's best kept secret." Without a doubt, getting the word out to potential business customers is a challenging task. SLCC learned that a sound marketing strategy can make a major difference. Possibly, some of the marketing practices identified in this article can help other community colleges promote their regions' "best kept secret."

Rand Johnson is director of the Advanced Technology Center at Salt Lake Community College, Utah.

PROCESS AUDITING TO ENHANCE THE MARKETING OF YOUR COMMUNITY COLLEGE

Wes Ellis

The Bevill Center for Advanced Manufacturing Technology, located on the campus of Gadsden State Community College in Gadsden, Alabama, devised a tool called the process audit that proved helpful in opening doors for industrial training and engineering problem solving. The process audit is offered as a free service to area companies and consists of a half-day, on-site review of corporate areas identified by companies as needing improvement. Individuals who are experts in the specific areas being reviewed perform the process audit and present the company with findings and recommendations that will improve the company's overall productivity and operations.

At the Bevill Center and other community college manufacturing technology centers, the process audit has resulted in an increase rate of training contracts with area businesses. The tool can easily be adapted for use by other community colleges that have technology resources and expertise. Here are the steps to performing a successful process audit:

**S A M P L E   P R O C E S S   A U D I T
P R O P O S A L   L E T T E R**

Mr. John Jones
Manager
ABC Manufacturing Company
Smalley, AL 22222

Dear Mr. Jones:

In an effort to assist industry in our region, The Bevill Center is offering free process audits to manufacturing companies in our area. The audits will be performed by one of our engineers specializing in your company's processes and will take approximately four hours, depending on the scope of investigation. The audit is not intended to tell managers how to run their operations, but rather to expose some areas of opportunities for improvement.

If you are interested, please contact me at 888-1234. Scheduling of the visit can be accomplished when you call. It will be helpful if you select a few areas of your plant where problems exist or where there may be room for improvement. If no such areas exist, a simple examination of your processes will be sufficient.

I look forward to hearing from you.

Sincerely,

Sally Smith
Business Liaison

1. Proposing the Process Audit

The first step in presenting and performing the audit is to propose the process audit to a company or companies in the region. This can be done through mailing a brochure and/or letter to area businesses. When preparing the proposal correspondence it is important to: (1) emphasize the value the process audit can be to the company; (2) explain that the length of the process audit is typically a half-day; (3) state that the audit will be performed by qualified staff who specialize in the company's field of expertise; and (4) emphasize the intention of the audit is not to tell managers how to run their company, but to identify some areas of opportunity exposed by a fresh perspective or point of view.

2. Select Area of Focus

Once a company agrees to have a process audit, the next step is to select specific corporate areas in which the experts should focus. This step should be done by company officials and not the experts. By preselecting focus areas, the company can pinpoint trouble points where benefits will be greatest. This also should help to avoid wasting time trying to identify problem areas during the audit.

3. Perform the Audit

When performing the audit, it is imperative that the audit be conducted by individuals with appropriate expertise for the process being reviewed. For example, if a company requests an audit of its computer-aided design (CAD) area, the person performing the audit must have superior knowledge about CAD systems and operations. The audit must be conducted in the time agreed upon by the community college staff and company personnel. During the process audit, the reviewer should identify areas where improvements can be made.

4. Report Results and Make Recommendations

After the audit is completed with company managers and/or employees, the results of the audit and recommendations are prepared and provided to the company. The report of findings should give technical descriptions of areas where there are opportunities for improvement. It should also request one or more of the recommendations be selected for immediate attention.

5. Follow-up with Proposals for Training Sessions

The final step of a successful process audit is to follow-up with the company by submitting proposals for training or engineering assistance in those areas identified as needing improvement. It is likely the company will choose the experts involved in the process audit as trainers because of the already established contact and rapport. As a result, the process audit serves as an effective mechanism for increasing business training contracts. The Bevill Center has found the process audit a successful method for establishing contacts and ongoing partnerships with area companies.

S A M P L E   R E P O R T   O F   F I N D I N G S

Computer-Aided Design (CAD) Area:

1. Investigation of this area showed great capability in the hardware and software used. However, it appeared that designers were under-utilizing those capabilities due to being "self taught" by experiences on the job.

2. This is a job shop. Designers in this area are creating new adaptions of the company's product for each product order. New designs are created without the benefit of communicating with the manufacturing floor to see if the new design can be built. There is no continuous flow of information to and from the shop floor.

Manufacturing Floor:

1. Equipment operators are required to use math skills in computing angles and measurements. Many of these calculations are incorrect, or must be calculated by the area supervisor before work can continue.

2. Labor is intensive in several areas, causing high costs in time and profits. There is machinery on the market that will perform these functions in a more automated fashion, freeing employees to be productive elsewhere.

Office Administration:

1. Computer hardware and software is fairly comprehensive here, but employees complain that many programs are too difficult to use. Others claim that the same programs are the best for the job. Little or no formal training has been performed in this area.

2. Scheduling of production lines on the shop floor is done by hand in this office. This employee rarely visits the shop floor and relies on production performance for finding mistakes or making changes in work scheduled.

SAMPLE RECOMMENDATIONS

Items:

1. At this stage in the company's maturity, collection and use of data from the manufacturing floor can be most helpful in planning and production. We recommend you first review and study data currently being reported, and the methods for gathering such data. You should then evaluate the various computer systems available for transferring manufacturing data from the floor to the plant mainframe computer system for compilation. We would be glad to assist your company in this effort.

2. Work flow analysis for the plant is recommended to investigate the possibilities for streamlining the manufacturing process and to reduce work in progress. It appeared that potential improvements existed. We will work with your staff and can recommend other agencies for handling the work flow study.

Recommendations:

1. Shop Floor Data Collection — the center will meet with appropriate personnel to discuss the content and scheduling of a project to complete the study, evaluation, and implementation of a system or systems to provide this technology. A proposal for such services will follow.

2. Work Floor Analysis — the center will propose a series of studies designed to enable managers to perform these operations themselves. This would be accomplished in conjunction with XYZ Center, whose staff is best equipped to perform the physical manufacturing floor work flow study.

Wes Ellis is industry relations/projects coordinator for the Bevill Center for Advanced Manufacturing Technology in Gadsden, Alabama.

I N T E R A C T I V E

M U L T I M E D I A   T R A I N I N G

David Dewhirst

usinesses and industries all across the country are savvy about the need for and benefits of a well-trained workforce. They are continually looking for better, more cost-effective ways to deliver training to their employees. In response to this need, InterACTive Information, Inc. developed InteracTV®, an interactive videodisc system that delivers performance-based training across geographically distributed networks. InteracTV® can benefit community colleges in delivering training to local business and industry.

InteracTV® is a multimedia delivery system for education and training in interactive form. It is geared for industrial organizations seeking: to communicate with or train individuals; to educate people at their own pace; to deliver training in a geographically dispersed area; to accommodate the trend toward mandated training; and to capitalize on advanced technology. Using audio, video, animation, graphic presentation, and text, InteracTV® creates interactive training that is implemented in an unsupervised, cost-effective manner. The outcome is improved comprehension and retention of course material.

The computer unit employs a touchscreen, not requiring a mouse, keyboard, or operating system. All it takes is a touch from the user. It can be used by anyone, even those who are not computer literate. InteracTV® focuses on training many people yet it treats the individual on a personal level. Course delivery can be adjusted to fit the pace of the student or employee who is taking the course because the learner is in control of the experience. A course can be automatically programmed to provide remedial material to the user or to progress to more advanced information.

ADVANTAGES OF INTERACTV®

Active Individualized Learning Process

- Trainee in control of experience
- Individualized instruction
- Improved retention of materials
- Ability to present complex concepts and situations
- Maintains trainee interest through audio and video interaction

Accessibility of Training Information

- Available all hours of the day and days of the week
- Automatic starting with no need for user knowledge of system operations
- Applicable to those with low literacy skills
- Multiple programs available at single station

Organized Administration of the System

- InterACTive Information Inc. performs all administration of courseware and documented results; no need for technical experts at each site
- Automatic accumulation of testing and questioning results
- Modification of course offerings as necessary through telephone communications
- No up-front costs

Community colleges can effectively utilize the InteracTV® system to provide diverse training to workers in small and medium-sized businesses. A pilot program is already underway, helping community colleges serve as local training centers. Since community colleges do not need to pay up-front capital costs, they can charge on a pay-per-view basis for all training provided. InterACTive Information, Inc., in conjunction with several established video training companies, will supply the courses and record all scores and documentation for the community college. InterACTive Information, Inc. can bill the company utilizing the training and pay the community college a royalty for its involvement.

A proprietary controller stores courseware programming, courseware, and the collection of training results. Using standard telephones lines, training results are collected and compiled for the instructors use. The InteracTV® system is supported by two additional software programs, one for creation of the branching code/storyboarding called the Course Creator, and the second for the management and collection of the distributed information from each of the off-site InteracTV® units referred to as the Network Manager. These proprietary products are key elements in InteracTV's overall functionality and efficiency.

The software Course Creator is based on visual language technology that permits the courseware creator to develop storyboards and courseware routing plans without the need for computer programming skills. This visual language system decreases computer coding time by more than 80 percent as compared to traditional text based coding methods.

The network manager software supports continuing courseware maintenance and report gathering from distributed InteracTV® units and allows courseware programming and service to be distributed nationwide via standard telephone lines.

InteracTV® provides better communication, instruction, and assessment at a lower cost than conventional methods. It provides the user with an active individualized learning process, maintains interest through audio and video interaction, and can be administered to those without prior computer skills. Interactive training courses include industrial safety, health and quality management and can be customized to meet customer needs. The system provides automatic tracking of student/employee performance and record keeping, enabling the successful training of large numbers of people in diverse geographical locations.

David Dewhirst is president of InterACTive Information, Inc. in Knoxville, Tennessee.

P R O V E N   S T R A T E G I E S

F O R   S T U D E N T   A N D   W O R K F O R C E

S U C C E S S

Cathy Webb, Marcia Heiman and Alan Lesure

The most important community and national asset is our people, our workforce. America's workers are the most productive in the world. However, as the needs of the workplace change, workers' ability to learn—to adapt effectively to new situations—is the only lasting source of a continuing competitive advantage. "Learn-how" has replaced "know-how" as the critical skill for the jobs of today and tomorrow.

What can be done for employees who were educated in a system that is inadequate for today's business needs? As educators, how do we ensure that graduates of our community and technical colleges will have the skills they need to continue to compete in an ever-changing work world?

What are the new skills required of workers?

Workplace Basics, a joint publication of the American Society for Training and Development and the U.S. Department of Labor, Employment and Training Administration, cites the importance of learning how to learn:

"Learning to learn...knowing how to learn—is the most basic of all skills because it is the key that unlocks future success. Equipped with this skill, an individual can achieve com-

STUDENT STUDY AT ROXBURY COMMUNITY COLLEGE

	Non-LTL Students (Received traditional remediation, including subject-matter tutoring)	LTL Students[2]
Retention in college semesters after intervention	40%	70%
Grade point average	2.22	2.89
# Credits completed in targeted semester	7.45	10.40

petency in all other basic workplace skills, from reading through leadership. Without this skill, learning is not as rapid nor as efficient and comprehensive."[1]

Based on this premise, an academic program has been developed called Learning to Learn® (LTL). LTL provides students with a set of analytical thinking skills that result in significant, long-term effects on students academic performance. LTL skills can be made available through colleges to workers and students.

Does Learning to Learn® make a difference with adult learners?

A government-validated study at Roxbury Community College, a two-year, open enrollment, public community college in Boston, Massachusetts, demonstrated that students who participated in the Learning to Learn® program were more likely to remain in school; had higher grade point averages; and completed more credits per semester than students who did not participate in the LTL courses.

[1] Anthony Carnevale, et al, *Workplace Basics: The Skills Employers Want*, pp. 8–9, 1988: Washington, D.C., American Society for Training and Development and the U.S. Department of Labor Employment and Training Administration.

[2] LTL data were validated by the U.S. Department of Education's Joint Dissemination Review Panel. The Department's LTL approval document number is JDRP No. 83-25. LTL's data show that the program benefits students at all levels, including educationally disadvantaged students and students who performed at the top of their class in high school.

READING SKILLS IMPROVEMENT AFTER 13 WEEKS OF TRAINING — 3 HOURS / WEEK *

	Workers Given Standard Remediation	LTL-Trained Workers
Workers with 8.0-8.9 reading levels	4.1 months reading gain	32.4 months gain
Workers with 9.0-9.9 reading levels	4.1 months reading gain	16.8 months gain

*The TABE reading inventory was used before and after both interventions.

Since January 1992, Meridian Community College (MCC) in Mississippi has used the academic version of Learning to Learn®, called *Success in College and Beyond*. It is a student textbook that shows students methods of questioning the world around them and helps them to learn and think more actively and effectively. MCC chose the academic version of LTL for three reasons:

1. The Learning to Learn® program provides excellent support for instructors. It includes an 800 number for faculty and trainers, trainers and teachers manuals, video support, faculty and trainer development programs of varying length, assessment instruments, and an evaluation procedure for the academic program.

2. LTL's organization is impressive; each part of the program reinforces other parts and the program is accessible and learnable to students.

3. The LTL program meets the needs of both academic and occupational learning.

In the past, MCC tried several other study skill programs, but none of them worked as consistently as Learning to Learn®. The success stories of students in the LTL program at MCC are numerous. One reason the program is so successful is that it teaches a system of related, inquiry-based skills, if correctly applied, ensure achievement. LTL skills are consistent with everything experts tell us about memory. To place information in long-term memory, the type of memory to be successful in college, students must work with new material in a variety of ways. The LTL system's skills require students to question information and use it in different forms and contexts. The result is efficient remembering.

What is Learning to Learn's Impact on Basic Skills?

Pre/post reading skills data were collected in a pilot LTL program given to workers at Eastman Kodak. A group was instructed in LTL's reading techniques. At the same time, a similar group of workers was given traditional reading remediation in a GED program. The students who received the LTL reading techniques made significantly better gains in their reading level than the students who received the traditional reading instructions.

Comparable results were found when Motorola conducted a controlled study of the effects of LTL's corporate program on 400 of its workers. Motorola's study measured participants' workplace performances on a number of indices, including problem solving, attention to detail, self-monitoring skills, learning readiness, analytical skills, orderliness and goal orientation. Compared with a control group, the assessment taken before and two months after LTL training showed that workers with Learning to Learn® skills performed better than the control group on all indices as assessed by the trainees, their co-workers, and their supervisors.

What is the Length and Scope of an LTL Program?

Results from studies reported in this article were obtained through faculty and trainer-based LTL classes delivered in college over a semester and in industry over a 13-week period, with classes lasting one to three hours. Similar LTL strategies were taught in all instances.

Today's student workers are too often undereducated and underprepared for the skills that will be required of them. America can regain its competitive edge if means are found to transform the workforce into employees who have learned how to learn. These are adults who:

- can readily comprehend technical information in educational and training programs and apply what they have learned;

- actively seek out new information;

- test themselves in new situations;

- demonstrate to themselves and others that they can solve problems as they arise.

Meridian Community College, Kirkwood Community College, Southside Virginia Community College and many others have learned what organizations such as Motorola, Eastman Kodak, Tandy Rank Video, and the U.S. Navy know. Learning to Learn® provides proven and learnable strategies and techniques that foster classroom competence and improved workplace performance.

This article is adapted from one that appeared in the Fall 1993 issue of the ATEA Journal.

Cathy Webb is LTL coordinator at Meridian Community College in Meridian, Mississippi; Marcia Heiman is co-president of Learning to Learn, Inc.; and Alan Lesure is president of Learning Resources, Inc. in Stamford, Connecticut.

RETRAINING THE
WORKFORCE: ONE COLLEGE'S
APPROACH

Rebecca Farrow

 o compete in the fast changing national and international markets, a well-trained workforce is an integral part of an organization's strategic plan. Successful employees function in a total quality environment with a foundation of basic skills, including critical thinking, problem solving and the ability to participate in a team-oriented workplace.

Richland College of the Dallas County Community College District has developed a video-based training program that provides a step-by-step process for implementing workplace literacy training programs. This tool is useful for professionals involved in business, industry, educational institutions, government agencies, and labor organizations.

Richland's system, containing six 30-minute videos, is designed to prepare businesses and organizations to upgrade workplace skills and empower employees to be the quality workforce of the future. Most importantly, this training approach allows employees to learn how to learn. Workplace literacy training may be what an organization needs to remain competitive in a global economy.

The system contains three primary parts:

- Six 30-minute videos, featuring case studies produced on-site in an actual work environment.

- Six training manuals containing hands-on learning experiences adaptable to a variety of business, industry and service environments.

- A facilitator's guide for training sessions.

The six training topics include:

1. *Marketing Workplace Literacy.* This component explains how workplace literacy differs from adult basic education, vocational education, adult literacy, and technical training. It describes typical program components and activities, anticipated timeliness, outcomes, and costs. In addition, it outlines marketing techniques for proposals to external or internal clients.

2. *Identifying Critical Job Tasks.* Describing value-added training, this section presents an instructional systems design approach to workplace literacy as well as the four levels of evaluation for determining effectiveness. It demonstrates how to identify and work with advisory committee members, identify needs and select critical job tasks. It also illustrates how to identify local performance indicators to measure program impact.

3. *Conducting Literacy Task Analyses.* This component prepares the trainer to expedite worksite investigations by previews of existing job descriptions, certification documentation and job materials. It lists hundreds of typical literacy tasks embedded in many jobs and demonstrates interview/observation session techniques.

4. *Designing Training Content.* Lesson components with instructional samples are presented in the fourth section of the Richland training program. It focuses on correct methods for introducing concepts, presenting new terms, modeling instructional concepts and guiding practice to enhance transfer of learning. It also teaches techniques that ensure testing for mastery of skill applications, not for technical knowledge. Recommendations for coordinating instruction time with production and work tasks are included.

5. *Implementing Assessment and Recruitment.* This component presents pros and cons for using basic skills tests in the workplace. It addresses the pros, cons, and required legal processes for creating, validating, and administering legal, customized worker-assessment instruments. Tips are also included for conducting orientation and public relations meetings with supervisors and employees.

6. *Measuring Program Effectiveness.* This final component of the video-based training describes how to measure a program against its own goals and provide timely information to program decision makers. It presents numerous data collection techniques, provides sample instruments, and specifies report content for use by various audiences. It also provides methods for giving staff constructive feedback and correcting problems.

Rebecca Farrow is director of Business and Industry Services at Richland College in Dallas, Texas.

THE WORKFORCE TRAINING IMPERATIVE

MEETING THE TRAINING NEEDS OF THE NATION—IMPLEMENTING A NATIONAL WORKFORCE TRAINING SYSTEM

Heart of the Ozarks Technical Community College in Missouri offers on-the-job-training for women in construction work. Photo credit: Susan Mumford

IMPLEMENTING A NATIONAL WORKFORCE TRAINING SYSTEM

his section is excerpted from *The Workforce Training Imperative: Meeting the Training Needs of the Nation, a Policy Paper on the Role of Community Colleges in Providing Workforce Training.* Developed jointly by the League for Innovation in the Community College and AACC, and adopted by AACC's Board of Directors in August 1993, the policy paper provides rationale for community colleges to serve as major providers of workforce training, particularly for unserved small and medium-sized companies located in their respective service areas. In order for this to occur as part of a coordinated national effort, the policy paper calls for all interested parties to work together to implement a plan for action. The following passage identifies what community colleges, business/industry communities, and local, state and federal governments must do to achieve a national workforce training system.

What Community Colleges Must Do:

- Community college leaders—trustees, CEOs, senior administrators, and faculty—should explicitly acknowledge that workforce training for employees of local business, industry, labor, and government is one of the core missions of their institutions, a logical extension of traditional career preparation, continuing education, and community service missions. They must acknowledge that providing training for individuals already in the workforce extends, but does not supplant, preparing new and returning entrants for the workforce.

- Community college leaders should develop organizational structures that bring workforce training into the mainstream of their institutions while retaining the flexibility to provide customer-driven training programs. Workforce training programs must co-exist alongside more traditional credit programs and receive comparable institutional support, while at the same time remaining free of the constraints of traditional programs, including academic schedules and credit-hour time requirements, lengthy curriculum review processes, negotiated contracts and faculty load and compensation requirements, and academic credential requirements for trainers.

- Community college leaders need to conduct ongoing staff development programs to educate their faculty about the needs and learning styles of adult workers, to learn about new delivery mechanisms and instructional methodologies for providing effective training for adults, and to update faculty skills continually so that they can be effective trainers for skills currently needed in the workplace.

- Community college leaders need to work with local business leaders to inform them of the workforce training programs and services that their colleges can provide to increase worker productivity and overall company competitiveness and profitability.

- Directors of community college workforce training programs need to work with supervisors and managers in business and industry and with their counterparts in community colleges nationwide to develop and share models for delivering effective workforce training, including alternative instructional delivery systems, model curricula in areas of high need, and flexible administrative and payment procedures.

- Community college leaders need to work with federal, state, and local government officials; elected representatives; and leaders of the corporate and small business community to develop policies and funding mechanisms at the local, state, and federal levels that provide incentives to business for investment in worker training and that ensure adequate funding for community colleges that provide workforce training as part of an overall economic development strategy.

- Community colleges should expand and implement their role as conveners in community coalitions in order to help forge better linkages among schools, government, employers, and community-based organizations.

- Community colleges should involve themselves in the development of skills standards in cooperation with government, business, industry, and other entities. Once these are developed, community colleges must respond to the challenges they will generate.

What Business and Industry Must Do:

- Business and industry leaders should explicitly acknowledge that workforce training is an unavoidable cost of doing business and of competing successfully in a global economy, and they must help educate their colleagues in business, industry, and labor of the need to invest in worker training.

- Business and industry leaders should work with local, state, and federal government officials to develop policies, programs, and incentives to encourage private investment in workforce training.

- Business and industry leaders should work with providers of training, including community colleges, to develop and implement models for effective workforce training at a reasonable cost and to validate these models by demonstrating that investment in training results in improved productivity and increased profitability.

- Employers should provide incentives to their employees to engage in continual upgrading of workplace skills.

What Local, State, and Federal Governments Must Do:

- The federal government should identify the expansion and improvement of workforce training and the upgrading of worker skills as the core of national economic strategy. The federal government must identify as a national priority the creation of a skilled and adaptable workforce that can compete successfully with any in the world.

- The federal government should take the leadership role in defining a coherent, customer-driven, results-oriented, workforce training system as part of a comprehensive national human investment policy that guides and supports state and local worker training and economic development efforts. Such a system should be built upon existing infrastructure at the state and local level, and it should explicitly identify community colleges as a major provider of workforce training both for those already employed and for new entrants into the workforce, especially for current employees of small and medium-sized businesses.

- The federal government should take the leadership role in developing broadly agreed-upon national standards for workforce competencies as a means of raising the skill levels of all American workers. These standards should guide the development and assessment of state-based and locally managed programs to improve workplace skills.

- Federal, state, and local governments should develop policies and regulations that provide incentives to employers to invest in workforce training and to employees to engage in continual skills updating. State and local officials, in particular, must review existing legislation, policies, and regulations to ensure that they neither discourage workforce training nor limit the workforce training mission of community colleges.

- State and local governments should develop funding mechanisms to support workforce training in areas of greatest need, including the use of public and private funds to support community college workplace training programs that serve the public interest as part of an overall economic development strategy.

- Federal, state, and local governments should develop incentives to support public-private partnerships, public-public partnerships such as community college-university collaborations, and other innovative financing arrangements to ensure that adequate resources are available to support workforce training, including programs that leverage public funds to attract private investment in support of workforce training.

Joint Responsibilities:

- Community college leaders, business and industry executives, and government officials need to work together to define a coherent system for providing workforce training. They need to acknowledge and value the roles that each has to play to ensure the expansion and improvement of workforce training in all types and sizes of organizations.

- Educators, business executives, politicians, the media, and other community leaders need to work to create a national climate and culture that establish the value of commitment to continuous quality improvement and to education and training as the foundation for both individual and national economic development.

NEW WORK
OCCUPATIONS

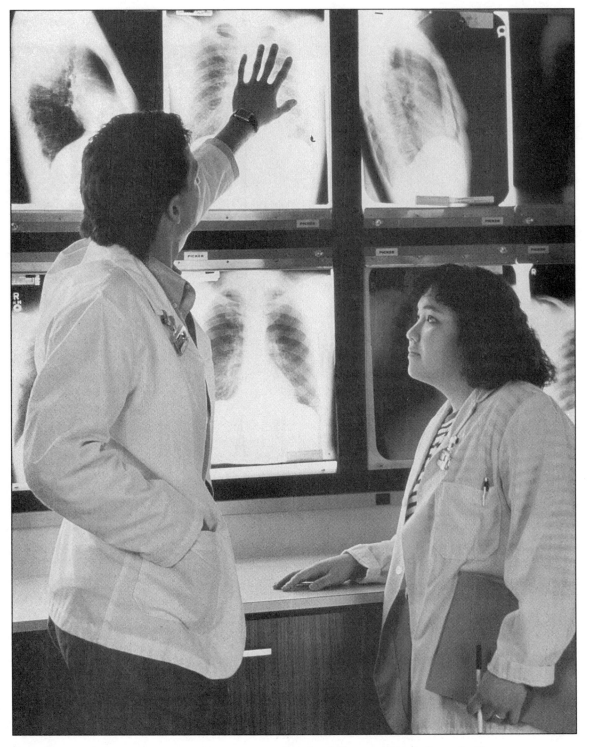

Instructor and student review x-ray images at Portland Community College in Oregon. Radiographer is an example of new work occupations. Photo credit: Jerome Hart

N E W   W O R K

O C C U P A T I O N S   C R I T E R I A

elected community colleges nationwide helped AACC and

the U.S. Department of Labor to identify existing examples

of "new work" occupations. Defined as emerging jobs that

command higher skills and pay higher wages, new work

occupations require workers with some postsecondary training, most typically a cer-

tificate or associate degree.

According to the U.S. Department of Labor Bureau of Labor Statistics, more than 121 million jobs exist in America today. By the year 2005, the projected number of jobs will grow to more than 147 million, resulting in a 22 percent total growth rate for all occupations. Using this number as a benchmark, the 35 occupations described in this publication were selected because they meet the new work definition and are expected to have at least an average growth rate through the year 2005. Some occupations, especially those in the medical field, can expect growth rates as high as 95 percent.

It should be noted that most new work occupations are not new. However, many have updated and upgraded skill requirements and all are considered to be jobs of the future. As the United States sees the demise of businesses and industries and the loss of numerous occupations that once were considered the nation's higher paying jobs, it is critical that the training offered by community colleges, or any service providers, results in employment and respectable wages.

The 35 occupations listed in this book are broadly categorized into seven fields:

- community service

- computer and information systems

- engineering, manufacturing and science

- environmental

- legal paraprofessional

- medical

- tourism and hospitality

The descriptions and training requirements for the occupations were developed from information provided by community colleges; the labor market information was verified using projections from the U.S. Department of Labor Bureau of Labor Statistics.

These occupations should not be misconstrued as the "best" occupations under the new work criteria. They are only a sample of the types of jobs that are projected to exist and grow through the year 2005. Community college workforce service providers are encouraged to investigate regional economic information before designing any new training programs.

Training workers for careers of tomorrow is the mission of the Advanced Technology Center at Luzerne County Community College in Pennsylvania. Photo credit: John Foglietta

NEW WORK OCCUPATIONS BY FIELDS

COMMUNITY SERVICE OCCUPATIONS

Community Law Enforcement Officer

Early Childhood Educator

Firefighter

COMPUTER AND INFORMATION SYSTEMS OCCUPATIONS

Computer Systems Analyst

Graphic Designer

Telecommunications and
Computer Network Manager

ENGINEERING, MANUFACTURING AND SCIENCE OCCUPATIONS

Automotive Service Technician

Composite Materials Technician

Computer-Aided Design Technician (CAD)

Computer-Integrated Manufacturing
Technician (CIM)

Computer Numerically Controlled
Operator (CNC)

Energy Technician

Engineering Technician

Laser Technician

Manufacturing Technician

Quality Control Technician

Robotics Technician

Science Technician

ENVIRONMENTAL OCCUPATIONS

Environmental Technician

Hazardous Waste Technician

Pollution Abatement
Technician

LEGAL PARAPROFESSIONAL OCCUPATIONS

Legal Assistant

Legal Secretary

MEDICAL OCCUPATIONS

Biomedical Equipment Technician

Dental Hygienist

Diagnostic Medical Sonographer

Emergency Medical Technician (EMT)

Medical Laboratory Technician

Medical Records Technician

Nurse

Physical Therapy Assistant

Radiologic Technologist
(Radiographer)

TOURISM AND HOSPITALITY OCCUPATIONS

Executive Chef

Hotel Manager

Travel Agent

COMMUNITY SERVICE OCCUPATIONS

Community Law Enforcement Officer

Description

Law enforcement officers are responsible for public safety and fighting crime. Responsibilities may vary greatly from traffic control to investigating serious criminal activities. Law enforcement officers may practice community policing, instructing the public in the best ways to help themselves and the police fight crime. Related positions are correctional officer, court officer, deputy sheriff, and security officer.

Skills

Police officers need a background in criminal justice with additional skills in computer science, psychology, sociology, and speech. They also must be able to use a firearm with accuracy, perform first aid, and drive an automobile at high speeds or under hazardous conditions.

Training

While some police departments will hire officers with only a high school diploma, more and more are requiring postsecondary education. Many community colleges offer law enforcement training, where instruction typically includes constitutional and criminal law, criminal evidence, court organization and procedures, first aid, defensive tactics, and firearms. In addition, courses may include counseling, sociology, and public relations.

Market Information

The employment outlook for police officers is expected to increase about as fast as the average for all occupations through the year 2005. The projected growth for correctional officers, a related occupation, is 70 percent. The average starting salary is $20,600 per year, but salaries and responsibilities can vary greatly depending on location and community size.

Early Childhood Educator

Family Day Care Provider
Director of Child Care Centers

Description

Early childhood development and education is a fast-growing career avenue that alleviates one of the most common and prominent barriers to bringing women into the workforce. Professional employment exists for family day care providers, early childhood educators and aides, teachers, and directors of licensed child care centers.

Skills

Competencies include: emergency first aid and fire safety procedures; curriculum development; knowledge of child development; excellent written and oral communication skills; excellent organizational, observation, record keeping, and accounting skills; knowledge of sound nutritional practices; and creativity, flexibility, and personal animation.

Training

Community colleges nationwide offer degree programs with both curriculum and site-based practicums.

Market Information

There has been a documented increase in the number of working women with children under the age of six. Businesses are finding that to attract and retain qualified individuals who are also parents, they must provide quality child care. This is currently being done in on-site centers or through partnerships with licensed facilities. To maintain the integrity of their work environment, many large employers are hiring their own qualified providers through accredited institutions. The number of jobs in early childhood education is expected to increase by 54 percent. Graduates from approved programs are earning starting salaries between $7.00 and $10.00 per hour.

Firefighter

Description

Firefighters respond to emergencies, control and extinguish fires, protect life and property, maintain equipment, and administer first aid and respiration to injured persons. Firefighters may be employed with industrial firms, governmental agencies, municipalities, and insurance companies.

Skills

A firefighter needs to be skilled in the principles and practical application of fire prevention, fire suppression, fire service management, and fire protection technology.

Training

Between one and two years training at a community college is typical training.

Market Information

The national demand is projected to be slightly lower than the average for all occupations. However, some regions of the country can expect average demand for this occupation. Starting salaries range from $1,000 to $1,500 per month.

COMPUTER AND INFORMATION SYSTEMS OCCUPATIONS

Computer Systems Analyst

Description

Systems analysts define business, scientific, or engineering problems, and design solutions using computers. They analyze the data processing requirements and plan new computer systems that will provide capabilities required for projected workloads. They may plan layout of a new system or may modify an existing system. The analysts work with the data processing and project managers to determine limitations and capabilities of an existing system and the projected workload. They evaluate factors (e.g. number of department serviced by the data processing equipment, volume of transactions, time requirements, cost restraints, and need for security and access restrictions) and then recommend and plan layouts for the new or modified system.

Skills

Skills in data processing, computer science, information science, or computer information are required. Analysts should have strong mechanical interest as well as an interest and willingness to learn programming. A background in mathematics and engineering is useful.

Training

At minimum, an associate degree from a community college is required. Some employers require a baccalaureate or graduate degree. Prior work experience is considered essential. Familiarity with programming languages and a broad knowledge of computer systems and technologies is required.

Labor Market

Employment in computer and data processing services is projected to grow 110 percent between 1992 and 2005. Starting salaries range between $23,000 and $25,000 per year.

Graphic Designer

Description

The position of graphic designer can vary from company to company, but typically the designer creates original art for newspapers, advertisements, magazines, newsletters, and/or books. Designers create the design and layout. Designers are responsible for developing cost estimates and preparing bids for evaluation by clients. They may be responsible for marketing their work to perspective clients. Many graphic designers are self-employed and/or work part-time.

Skills

The skills needed by graphic designers are: creativity; ability to function effectively while meeting deadlines; ability to operate a computer using word processing, spreadsheet cost analysis, and computer graphics; knowledge of layout techniques and printing; and excellent communication skills to sell ideas and final products to clients. Talent and originality are important for success.

Training

Graphic designers can receive training in art schools, community colleges, or universities. Experience and a portfolio are important to obtaining a job in this field.

Market Information

Nationally, the occupation is expected to grow faster than the average through the year 2005. Employment is very competitive; the supply of workers exceeds the need. The average starting salary is $1,310 per month and experienced graphic designers average $2,465 per month.

Telecommunications and Computer Network Manager

Description

Telecommunications and network managers are responsible for preparing, installing, and maintaining the local area computer network of the company. They teach employees to use the system, install new systems as needs are determined, and are responsible for diagnosing and resolving network software problems.

Skills

The manager needs: the ability to evaluate network hardware and software packages; knowledge of the latest technology as well as existing common carriers (telephones, networks, radio); and an understanding of appropriate laws that relate to local and federal communications environment. A strong background in math, basic computer programming, and/or engineering is necessary.

Training

Most employers look for an associate degree in computer science with an emphasis in computer networking and telecommunications. Specific courses are required in telecommunications, networking, software engineering, operation systems, and cooperative work experience.

Market Information

This occupation is projected to be one of the fastest growing industries in the United States through 2005. Network managers will be especially valuable to small and medium-sized businesses. The starting salary range is between $23,000 and $40,000.

ENGINEERING, MANUFACTURING AND SCIENCE OCCUPATIONS

Automotive Service Technician

Description

Automotive service technicians repair, service, and adjust mechanical and electrical parts of automobiles, trucks, recreational vehicles, buses, tractors, and other gasoline-powered equipment. They perform preventive maintenance, diagnose trouble, make adjustments, estimate costs, repair or replace defective parts, rebuild assemblies, and test all repairs to insure proper operation. Specializations may include engine repair, automatic transmissions, manual transmissions and rear axle, front suspension, brakes, electrical systems, heating and air conditioning, and engine tune-up and emission.

Skills

In addition to fundamental mechanical and electrical knowledge, automotive technicians require good analytical and communication skills, and a thorough knowledge of specific equipment.

Training

Certificates and associate degrees are available from community colleges.

Market Information

The employment outlook for automotive technicians is slightly higher than average through 2005. This is due to the growing number of vehicles being operated in the United States, the opening of new repair shops and garages, the trend of consumers to keep vehicles longer, and changing federal and state regulations covering vehicle safety inspections and pollution control. The salary range is between $20,000 and $50,000.

Composite Materials Technician

Description

Materials are being engineered and created to replace metals, synthetics, and other production materials not suited for advanced manufacturing technologies. Materials utilization technicians are trained to work with amorphous and polymer materials and others that may be produced at the molecular level through the process of molecular beam epitaxy, involving atomic crystal growth. In addition, technicians may be trained to work with genetically engineered organic materials. These and other man-made materials will be substituted for natural-element metals and materials now being depleted.

Skills

Technicians need a background in metallurgy, materials science and chemistry.

Training

Two years of college is expected by most employers. Community colleges offer classroom and laboratory instruction supplemented by on-site internships.

Market Information

In 1993, there were 500,000 jobs available in the United States.

Computer-Aided Design (CAD) Technician

Description

CAD technicians operate computers to draft layouts, line drawings and designs. They produce and modify drawings by typing commands on a keyboard and using a light pen on the screen, or use a digitizer to draw, change or delete the designs. CAD technicians work in every industry that requires drawings such as architectural firms, automotive manufacturers, electronics firms, and the aerospace industry. Strong background skills in drafting and computer science are required.

Skills

CAD technicians need knowledge of drafting terminology; basic drafting skills; the ability to operate equipment and produce drawings; creativity; an attention to detail; and a high level of concentration and accuracy.

Training

There is no required certification. Training takes between one and two years at a community college, with specific training in programming CAD systems.

Market Information

Employment of CAD technicians is expected to grow 25 to 34 percent through the year 2005. The starting salary is between $18,000 and $29,000.

Computer-Integrated Manufacturing (CIM) Technician

Description

CIM technicians work and function in a totally automated factory in which all manufacturing processes are integrated and controlled by a computer-aided design and computer-aided manufacturing (CAD/CAM) system. The technician understands all the operations in the manufacturing plant and may work as part of management.

Skills

CIM technicians need to know the components and integration of the various technologies in robotics, CAD, and computer numerically control (CNC) machines. These may include machine tool usages, work cell development, machine downloading practices, post processor development, material handling, applications of statistical process control, system monitoring and data collection, networking work cell systems, and small and large-plant CIM applications.

Training

An associate degree of applied science from a community college is typical training.

Market Information

This is a fairly new position that is expected to be in demand in the next decade. The salary range is projected to be $23,000 to $40,000.

Computer Numerically Controlled (CNC) Operator

Description

The CNC operator works for a manufacturing company that typically produces a number of products using numerically controlled equipment. The electronics, medical instrumentation, transportation, communication, and computer industries typically use these operators. The CNC operator produces finished, high quality, low tolerance products through a process that transfers computer generated designs into cutting and shaping operations.

Skills

The CNC operator is capable of: setting up various fixtures and holding devices on the machine tool; selecting proper tooling; understanding the theories of machining, metals and cutting tools; performing programming in CNC languages; loading programs; and writing programs at the controller level. Critical thinking, basic math, and problem solving skills are necessary.

Training

Typically, much of the training is on-the-job with employees progressing from basic to more advance machining. Competency-based degree programs are also available at community colleges.

Market Information

This is an emerging position that is expected to increase in demand. Jobs can be found in manufacturing companies, particularly those companies with 50 or fewer employees. The salary range is $8.00 to $16.00 per hour.

Energy Technician

Description

Energy technicians will be needed in nuclear power plants; coal, shale, and tar sands extraction, processing and distribution; solar systems manufacturing, installation, and maintenance; synfuels production; biomass facilities operations; and possibly geothermal and ocean thermal energy conversion operations.

Skills

Technicians need a strong background in chemistry, earth science, and biology. In addition, they need good communication skills and math skills, including a knowledge of algebra, trigonometry, and basic physics.

Training

A minimum of two years of college is required by most employers. Community colleges offer programs utilizing classroom and laboratory training. On-site internships are recommended for gaining direct work experience.

Market Information

In 1993, there were 1.5 million jobs available in the United States. The average annual salary is estimated to be $26,000.

Engineering Technician

Description

Engineering technicians use the principles and theories of science, engineering and mathematics to solve problems in research and development, manufacturing, sales, construction and customer service. Their jobs are more limited in scope and more practically oriented than those of scientists and engineers. Many engineering technicians assist engineers and scientists, especially in research and development. Others work in production or inspection jobs. Technicians in research and development may build or set up equipment, prepare and conduct experiments, calculate or record results. Manufacturing engineering technicians may prepare specifications for materials, devise and run tests to ensure product quality, or study ways to improve manufacturing efficiency. Civil engineering technicians may assist civil engineers plan and build highways, buildings, bridges, dams and other structures, and do related surveys and studies.

Skills

Engineering technicians need to have a strong aptitude for the physical sciences, engineering, and mathematics. They also need general skills of accuracy, attention to detail, and precision.

Training

Most employers prefer to hire someone who will require less on-the-job training and supervision, although it is possible to acquire some positions with no formal training. Associate degree programs at community colleges that offer a combination of technical background and theory are a good point of entry into the field and allow acceptance at a four-year institution.

Market Information

Job outlook is best for electrical and electronic engineering technicians. In 1991, average annual starting salary was $20,400. Senior positions averaged $38,800.

Laser Technician

Description

Laser technicians assemble, test, maintain, and operate various laser devices and systems. They conduct tests and measurements using electronic devices and report the results to the engineering personnel. They work in research laboratories of companies that manufacture lasers and precision equipment.

Skills

The technician needs: an ability to manipulate, operate and adjust all elements of a laser device; the understanding of the nature of power supplies, mirrors, and various active media; and the ability to communicate effectively with engineers, physicians, scientists, and other users and designers in written reports and oral presentations.

Training

Associate degrees are required. Courses should be taken in math, physics, electronic instrumentation and calibration, electro-mechanical controls, lasers, digital circuits, and microwaves. Completion of a electronics program with additional courses in laser technology would also qualify one to work as a laser technician.

Market Information

Due to the increase in laser use, employment for laser technicians is expected to grow 25 to 34 percent through the year 2005. Annual salaries range from $23,000 to $35,000.

Manufacturing Technician

Description

Manufacturers are increasingly utilizing production work cells to enable optimal production flexibility and efficiency. As a result, a new role is emerging for manufacturing technicians. These technicians perform a wide variety of manufacturing operations such as drilling, milling, and quality control. They determine the most cost-effective sequence of operations. Technicians are likely to work with a team.

Skills

Manufacturing technicians need basic skills in math, communication, production, and teamwork. They need the ability to solve problems and think critically; knowledge of principles of total quality management; computer application skills; ability to interpret schematic drawings; knowledge of industrial control systems; flexibility, and initiative.

Training
Programs are offered at community colleges and typically include both classroom and work-based learning.

Market Information
The estimated salary range is $18,000 to $30,000.

Quality Control Technician

Description
Quality control technicians test and inspect products in various stages of production and collect data to determine quality of products. They evaluate data and reports, using statistical quality control procedures. Technicians write reports and make suggestions for modification of standards to achieve optimum quality. Technicians may specialize in a specific area of quality control engineering. Examples of products that may be tested include food, clothing, glassware and automobiles.

Skills
These technicians need a knowledge of mathematics, the ability to see slight differences in objects and shapes, written communication skills, a knowledge of the standards for a specific product, and patience and precision.

Training
Although there are no specific requirements for training, there are community colleges that offer certificates and associate degrees.

Market Information
Employment is best for those technicians specializing in food products. Starting salary range is between $12,000 and $18,500 per year.

Robotics Technician

Description
Robotics technicians assist robotics engineers in various tasks related to the design, development, production, testing, operation, repair, and maintenance of robots and robotics devices. They program robots to do their tasks.

Skills
Robotics technicians need excellent mechanical aptitude and hand-eye coordination. They must be methodical thinkers, independent, and team players. They need to possess related technical skills.

Training

Most employers require an associate degree, though there is no special licensing required. Courses should include basic engineering, electronics robot programming, and industrial robotics. Manufacturing technology is a common course of study.

Market Information

Employment of robotics technicians is expected to grow 25 to 34 percent through the year 2005. Starting salary ranges from $22,000 to $29,000.

Science Technician (Agricultural, Biological, Chemical, Nuclear and Petroleum)

Description

Science technicians use the principles and theories of science and mathematics to solve problems in research and development, and to investigate, invent, and help improve products. Their jobs are more practically oriented than those of scientists. Recently, laboratory instrumentation and procedures have become more complex, changing the nature of the work for technicians in research and development. The increasing use of robotics to perform many routine tasks formerly done by technicians has freed technicians to operate more sophisticated laboratory equipment. Science technicians make extensive use of computers, robotics, and high-technology industrial applications such as biological engineering.

Technicians set up, operate, and maintain laboratory instruments; monitor experiments; calculate and record results; and often develop conclusions. Included in this category are agricultural, biological, chemical, nuclear, and petroleum technicians.

Skills

A strong background in science and math courses at the high school level is important for entry into this field. Technicians also need excellent communication skills, an ability to work as part of a team, and computer skills.

Training

Most employers prefer applicants who have an associate degree from a community college in a specific technology or general math and science education.

Market Information

The projected growth rate for all science occupations is 25 percent. The employment of biological technicians is expected to grow faster than most other science technicians. The average annual salary is $24,700.

ENVIRONMENTAL OCCUPATIONS

Environmental Technician

Description

Environmental technicians conduct tests and field work to obtain data for use by environmental scientists. Through chemical and physical laboratory field tests, they determine sources of contamination to air, water, and soil; summarize the findings; and make recommendations for controlling pollutants.

Skills

The technician needs: an understanding of ecosystems, pollution control actions, hazardous waste, and toxic materials; surveying and mapping abilities; strong math and science skills; excellent written and oral communication skills; and knowledge of government regulations related to the environment.

Training

Training can range from one to four years at a postsecondary institution. Specific courses should be taken in regulatory waste management. Most programs offer classroom and laboratory instruction as well as on-the-job training through internships.

Market Information

Due to new regulations and heightened awareness of the ecological crisis facing various regions of the country, there is a shortage of skilled technicians in the environmental technology field. Most graduates have obtained employment with private sector environmental consulting agencies, service companies, and local, state, and regional environmental agencies. The starting salary is between $18,000 to $30,000.

Hazardous Waste Technician

Description

Hazardous waste technicians manage hazardous materials and waste in compliance with local, state, and federal regulations. They work in a variety of settings to manage the waste produced in processing and manufacturing. They may handle, store, transport, and destroy materials. Technicians work closely with professional staff (engineers and managers) to protect human health and the environment, and to minimize an organization's risk.

Skills

Hazardous waste technicians need to be proficient in collecting, analyzing, and disposing of radioactive, toxic, and waste materials. They must have knowledge of chemistry, applied physics, safety procedures, storage systems, government regulations, industrial processing, storing technology, and transportation regulations. Technicians need to know the chemical and physical properties of waste products as unique to specific industries.

Training

Most employers require an associate degree in chemical technology or waste management through a community college. Technicians will need continuing education on government regulations as appropriate to the industry.

Market Information

The demand for hazardous waste technicians is great and is expected to grow through the year 2005. Many hazardous waste technicians currently work for the federal government, but this situation should change as companies begin to look for ways to save money and limit their liability. Starting annual salaries range between $16,000 and $21,000. After three to five years experience, salaries range from $25,000 to $30,000 per year.

Pollution Abatement Technician

Treatment Plant Operator
Laboratory Technician
Wastewater Treatment Consultant
Industry Sales Representative

Description

The pollution abatement technology field is designed to offer career options for well-trained personnel in a variety of specialized positions in the water pollution control field. Graduates of pollution abatement education programs can pursue careers in the public and private sectors as treatment plant operators, laboratory technicians, wastewater treatment consultants, and industry sales representatives.

Skills

Competencies include a background in math and science, excellent reading comprehension, solid writing skills, and a demonstrated strength in analytical and diagnostic skills.

Training

Community colleges offer programs with classroom and laboratory instruction. Students are often encouraged to do an on-site internship at a treatment facility.

Market Information

Water pollution abatement standards have become increasingly more stringent. The thrust for clean water has led to the construction and upgrading of treatment facilities throughout the nation. This activity has generated a significant demand for wastewater treatment personnel. The salary for pollution abatement varies greatly depending on public or private employers. The starting salary range is $18,000 to $25,000 per year.

LEGAL PARAPROFESSIONAL OCCUPATIONS

Legal Assistant

Description

Legal assistants work as paraprofessionals to attorneys, providing assistance by researching law, investigating facts, and preparing documents. They use law sources, including statutes and legal decisions to develop legal documents, correspondence and memos. Legal assistants may specialize in one area of the law or may coordinate activities of the law office, including financial records.

Skills

Legal assistants need the ability to write, organize, read complex materials, research, interview and investigate. They must have a knowledge of legal terms, a familiarity with a specialty area such as litigation or corporate law, and an understanding of the court system. The ability to balance a variety of tasks is important, and they may need skills in law office systems management.

Training

Employers prefer to hire graduates of community college training programs. Training is also offered by four-year colleges and universities and law schools. The quality of training programs vary. Applicants should look for programs that are approved by the American Bar Association.

Market Information

The projected growth rate for this occupation is 86 percent. Lawyers are delegating more tasks to legal assistants. Competition for positions is intense. Nationally, the average starting salary is $1,665 per month, but wages vary depending on location.

Legal Secretary

Description

Legal secretaries prepare legal documents and correspondence including summonses, complaints, motions, and subpoenas under the supervision of a lawyer. They review law journals and assist in legal research. They answer telephones, greet clients, schedule appointments, file, complete forms, operate office machines, and other clerical tasks. Some may record testimonies and proceeding of meetings and conventions, handle office bookkeeping, serve as office manager, and oversee the law library.

Training

Vocational technical schools offer a legal secretary certification. Community colleges offer certification and/or degrees in business, office, and general secretarial programs.

Market Information

Employment of legal secretaries is expected to grow 57 percent through the year 2005. Annual salaries range from $19,000 to $33,000. Salaries are contingent upon size and location of the law firm.

MEDICAL OCCUPATIONS

Biomedical Equipment Technician

Description

The biomedical equipment technician repairs, installs, and maintains medical equipment used in hospitals, research universities, and private research facilities. Examples of equipment serviced are patient monitors, electrocardiographs, x-ray units, and other related technical equipment. A related position is biomedical equipment salesperson.

Skills

Biomedical repair technicians must understand medical terminology, principles, and practices; work with tools to repair and install equipment; complete equipment documentation forms; and teach staff to use equipment.

Training

A certificate can be obtained in one to two years at a community college. Courses in laser physics, fiber optics, electronics, and medical terminology are typically required.

Market Information

The projected employment opportunities are about average. The starting salary is $17,000 to $21,000 per year.

Dental Hygienist

Description

Dental hygienists provide preventive dental care and teach patients how to practice good oral hygiene. They examine patients' teeth and mouth and record the presence of diseases and abnormalities. They also administer local anesthetics and nitrous oxide/oxygen analgesia, and place and carve filling materials.

Skills

Hygienists should work well with others, particularly patients who are under stress. Dental hygienists must have manual dexterity, because they use dental instruments with little room for error in a patient's mouth. Hygienists must have knowledge in anatomy, physiology, chemistry, microbiology, pharmacology, nutrition, radiography, histology, periodontology, pathology, dental materials, clinical dental hygiene, and social and behavioral sciences.

Training

Licensure by the state in which hygienists practice is required. To qualify for licensure, a candidate must graduate from an accredited dental hygiene school and pass both a written and clinical examination. Completion of an association degree program is sufficient for practice in a private dental office. A bachelor or advanced degree is usually required for positions that involve research, teaching, or clinical practice in public or school health programs. The course of study will include laboratory, clinical, and classroom instruction.

Market Information

Employment for dental hygienists is expected to grow 43 percent through the year 2005. The average annual salary for dental hygienists is $36,400, and the average starting salary is $31,616.

Diagnostic Medical Sonographer (Ultrasound Technologist)

Description

Sonographers provide patient services under the direction of a physician using diagnostic ultrasound equipment. They select equipment for use during the examination; explain procedures and help the patient assume position for the examination; operate the ultrasound equipment; and present and discuss results with the physician.

Skills

Sonography is a highly skilled allied health profession, requiring excellent judgment and the ability to be sensitive to the patient's needs. The sonographer needs to perform sonographic scans on patients, interpret sonographic data, review and record patient history and appropriate clinical data, and recognize both normal and abnormal factors in sonographic visualization of internal body parts.

Training

A certificate of achievement or an associate degree of applied science from a postsecondary institution is required.

Market Information

The projected growth rate for this position is better than average. Starting salary ranges from $8.00 to $15.00 per hour.

Emergency Medical Technician (EMT-Paramedic)

Description

Emergency medical technicians provide pre-hospital care under medical command authority to acutely ill or injured patients and/or transport patients by ambulance or other emergency vehicles. They give first aid and other medical care to stabilize the patient's condition. They also maintain the ambulance and medical equipment and write reports. EMTs work in conjunction with physicians, nurses, and other health care professionals.

Skills

In addition to fundamental knowledge of human anatomy/physiology and basic sciences, EMT-paramedics should possess awareness of their abilities and limitations, the ability to relate to people, and the capacity to make rational patient-care decisions under stress.

Training

All EMTs must be certified. Associate degrees are available at community colleges. Some EMTs work as volunteers to gain experience.

Market Information

Employment growth is projected to be 36 percent through the year 2005. EMTs are often employed by municipal fire departments. Average entry wage is $1,805 per month.

Medical Laboratory Technician

Description

Medical laboratory technicians work as paraprofessionals to a medical technologist. They perform routine tests in the medical laboratory to provide data for use in diagnosis and treatment of disease. They may prepare specimens and operate automatic analyzers. Technicians may specialize or work in a variety of areas of the clinical laboratory.

Skills

Entry level skills include: a strong background in medical laboratory techniques in the areas of hematology, chemistry, microbiology, urinalysis, immunology, and blood banking; a knowledge of human anatomy and physiology; good communication skills; and the ability to be sensitive to the needs of patients.

Training

An associate degree or certificate from a community college or vocational program is typically required. Some states require licensure.

Market Information

The employment outlook for medical laboratory technicians is excellent in all regions of the country, with employment growth projected to be 26 percent. An aging population and advances in biotechnology contribute to the increase in laboratory testing. Entry level salary range is $8.00 to $12.00 per hour.

Medical Records Technician

Description

Medical records technicians organize, analyze, and technically evaluate health information; compile various administrative and health statistics; and code diseases, operations, procedures, and other therapies. They maintain and use a variety of health information indexes, special registries, storage and retrieval systems; input and retrieve computerized health data. They control the use and release of health information.

Skills

The successful medical records technician must have a team orientation, be articulate, have excellent business skills, and be computer literate. Contact with the general public is not common, but frequent communication with insurance representatives and other hospital personnel is predictable.

Training

The typical route of training is an associate degree, or a home-study program administered by the American Health Information Management Association. The Accredited Records Technician (ART) national credential is a desired outcome of training.

Market Information

Employment of medical records technicians is expected to grow 61 percent through the year 2005. Opportunities exist within hospitals, medical group practices, health maintenance organizations, nursing homes, clinics, and insurance firms. Annual salaries for technicians range between $17,000 and $33,900. Technicians with the ART earn $2,000 to $3,000 more annually.

Nurse (Associate of Applied Science Degree)

Description

Nurses administer impatient nursing and rehabilitation and health related personal care to patients with various need levels. They provide treatment to ill or injured persons under the instructions of a physician.

Skills

Nurses need: a strong desire to help others; genuine concern for the welfare of patients and clients; an ability to deal with difficult people and stressful situations; and a knowledge of math, biology, microbiology, chemistry, anatomy, and physiology.

Training

Employers require an associate of applied science degree from a community college. Training time can range between two and four years. State license exam is required.

Market Information

Employment in nursing is projected to grow 42 percent through 2005. Salaries are contingent upon size of hospital and geographic location, with a range of $22,000 to $39,000.

Physical Therapy Assistant (PTA)

Description

A PTA is involved in the following duties: assisting the physical therapist in planning therapy programs for patients; giving patients massages and heat treatments; helping patients improve their mobility through a variety of modalities; teaching patients to use artificial limbs, and braces; caring for therapy equipment such as exercise machines and whirlpools; and keeping records and reports of patients' care and progress.

Skills

PTAs should be in good physical condition, because they may have to lift and support patients during exercise and treatment. They need an interest in working with people, patience in dealing with people who may be under stress, and an ability to communicate effectively with all age groups.

Training

The community college associate of applied science degree is required for physical therapy assistants. Courses may include human biology, psychology, structural kinesiology, and therapeutic procedures. Classroom and laboratory work are supplemented by clinical placements in health care settings, where students work under the supervision of a physical therapist. State licensure is required.

Market Information

Employment for physical therapy assistants is expected to grow 93 percent through the year 2005. Growth will continue as new technologies save more people, who will need therapy. The salary range is $22,000 to $28,000.

Radiologic Technologist (Radiographer)

Description

Radiographers operate radiologic equipment to produce x-rays to be used for diagnostic purposes. They work with physicians in administering to patients chemical mixtures that enhance the visibility of certain organs or anatomical parts. Radiographers explain the procedure to the patient and assists in positioning the patient. They work under the direction of radiologists in a healthcare setting. A related occupation is radiation therapy technologist.

Skills

Radiographers need a fundamental knowledge of chemistry, human anatomy and physiology, medical terminology, and a specific proficiency in radiobiology and radiographic physics.

Training

Training programs are offered through community colleges, hospitals, medical centers, colleges and universities. Associate degree programs consist of classroom instruction and clinical experience. The classroom curriculum encompasses both general education, including mathematics, speech, composition, and basic science, and job-specific courses, including radiographic positioning, radiographic pathology, and administration. Some states require licensing.

Market Information

Employment in radiology technology is expected to grow 63 percent. The average starting salary is $18,408. There are opportunities to work part-time in this field.

TOURISM AND HOSPITALITY OCCUPATIONS

Executive Chef

Description

Executive chefs are responsible for the overall planning, production, and presentation of all foods and nonalcoholic beverages in a food service facility. They select and train the cooks and direct their daily work. As supervisors, chefs motivate and broaden cooks' horizons. They are active in public relations and marketing the establishment. Chefs carefully control costs to insure profitability. As part of the management team, they work with other department heads to plan and execute goals and objectives.

Skills

Chefs must possess a practice and knowledge of safety and sanitation, equipment and operation, food preparation, and food purchasing and storage. They need to be proficient in customer relations, management, and communication skills.

Training

Degrees in culinary management are awarded by community colleges. Apprenticeships offer entry into the field. Typical students graduate with the skills to become certified cooks through the American Culinary Federation. To progress, one must have a combination of professional experience, continued education, and involvement with the American Culinary Federation.

Market Information

With the growth in the hospitality industry, the need for quality chefs is increasing. The projected growth rate for this occupation is 35 percent. Starting salary is between $18,000 to $25,000 per year.

Hotel Manager

Description

Hotel managers/assistant managers are responsible for the operations of the hotel, and for its efficiency and profitability. They must ensure the guest's stay is as enjoyable as possible. In small hotels a single manager may oversee all aspects of operations. In large hotels, it is likely a manager will direct a specific area of the hotel such as front office, house-keeping, food/beverage, or conventions.

Skills

Hotel managers must have the ability to get along well with others, even in stressful situations, and to organize and direct the work of others. They must be able to solve problems and deal effectively with details.

Training

While it is possible to be promoted through the ranks to assistant manager or manager with only a high school diploma, postsecondary training in hotel and restaurant management is typically preferred by employers. Graduates of an associate degree program are likely to find employment as trainee assistant managers. Some four-year colleges also offer degree programs. Most employers prefer experience working in a hotel or restaurant.

Market Information

The growth rate for positions in hotel management is 44 percent. Salaries vary greatly in this field, depending on size of hotel, level of responsibility, and experience. Assistant managers earn between $23,000 and $40,000.

Travel Agent

Description

Travel agents work in such areas as ticketing, reservations, and tour planning. They often talk over the phone with clients making arrangements for transportation, hotel accommodations, car rentals, and recreational activities. Travel agents work long hours, particularly during vacation seasons. Many travel agents are self-employed.

Skills

Travel agents need a thorough understanding of the travel industry, excellent communication skills, and an attention for details. Ability to speak foreign languages is useful. Self-employed travel agents need a background in accounting and business management.

Training

Since fewer agencies are willing to train agents on-the-job, specialized training is becoming more important. Community colleges award certificates and associate degrees in travel and tourism.

Market Information

Travel agent positions are expected to increase by 66 percent through the year 2005. Starting salary is $12,000 per year, with experienced agents receiving $21,000 to $25,000.

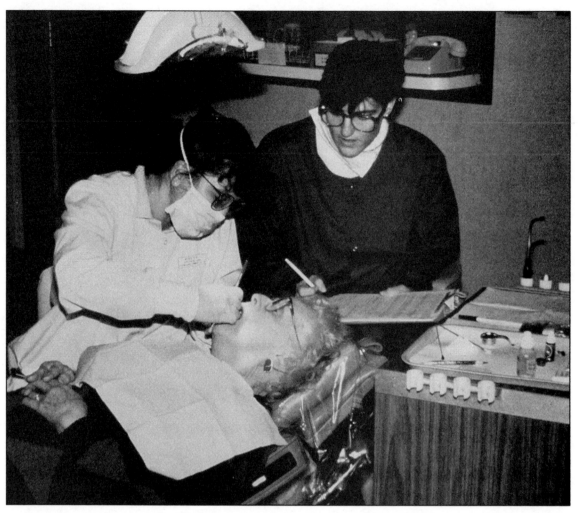

Luzerne County Community College in Pennsylvania trains students to become dental hygienists, an occupation predicted to increase in demand by 43 percent through 2005. Photo credit:
John Foglietta

Community Colleges Contributing Information about New Work Occupations

Central Virginia Community College, VA

Cincinnati Technical College, OH

College of DuPage, IL

College of Lake County, IL

Collin County Community College, TX

Community College of Allegheny County, PA

Community College at Jacksonville, FL

Dundalk Community College, MD

Florida Community College at Jacksonville, FL

Hinds Community College, MS

Jackson Community College, MI

Johnson County Community College, KS

Kirkwood Community College, IA

LaGuardia Community College, NY

Lake Michigan College, MI

Macomb Community College, MI

Mesa Community College, AZ

North Iowa Area Community College, IA

Okaloosa-Walton Community College, FL

Pima County Community College District, AZ

San Diego Community College District, CA

J. Sargeant Reynolds Community College, VA

Shoreline Community College, WA

Sinclair Community College, OH

Southern Maine Technical College, ME

Springfield Technical Community College, MA

State Center Community College District, CA

Tri-County Technical College, SC

Tulsa Junior College, OK

SELECTED REFERENCES

American Association of Community Colleges. *The Workforce Training Imperative: Meeting the Needs of the Nation.* Washington, D.C.: American Association of Community Colleges, 1993.

Carnevale, Anthony P., Leila J. Gainer, and A. Meltzer. *Workplace Basics: The Skills Employers Want.* Washington, D.C.: U.S. Department of Labor and American Society for Training and Development, 1989.

Carnevale, Anthony P. and Leila J. Gainer. *The Learning Enterprise.* Alexandria, Va.: The American Society for Training and Development, 1989.

Commission on the Skills of the American Workforce. *America's Choice: High Skills or Low Wages!* Rochester, N.Y.: National Center on Education and the Economy, 1990.

Dilcher, Ann Katherine. *Learning that Works: The Provision of Workplace Education by Community Colleges.* Washington, D.C.: American Association of Community Colleges and the Southport Institute for Policy Analysis, 1993.

Doucette, Don. *Community College Workforce Training Programs for Employees of Business, Industry, Labor, and Government: A Status Report.* Mission Viejo, Calif.: League for Innovation in the Community College, 1993.

Heiman, Marcia, and Joshua Slomianko. *Success in College and Beyond.* Allston, MA: Learning to Learn, Inc., 1992.

Jacobs, James. *Customized Training in Michigan: A Necessary Priority for Community Colleges.* Warren, Mich.: Macomb Community College, 1992.

Texas Innovation Network and The Texas Department of Commerce. *Technology and Emerging Occupations.* Dallas, TX: Texas Innovation Network, Second edition, 1992.

U.S. Department of Labor. *Occupational Outlook Handbook*. Lincolnwood, IL: VGM Career Horizons, NTC Publishing Group, 1988–89 ed.

U.S. Department of Labor Bureau of Labor Statistics. *Monthly Labor Review*. Washington, D.C.: U.S. Government Printing Office, November 1993.

U.S. Employment Service. *Directory of Occupational Titles*. Fourth Edition, volumes 1 and 2, U.S. Government Printing Office, Revised 1991.

INDEX